The Ultimate Guide to SAT Grammar 2nd Edition

Erica L. Meltzer

ISBN-13: 978-1492353294
ISBN-10: 1492353299

DEDICATION

To Emma and Joey, for whom these exercises were first written. I know you probably don't want a grammar book dedicated to you, but I hope you'll accept the gesture. And to Jane, Joe, Lily, and Frisco, for food, company, inspiration, and hilarity.

CONTENTS

INTRODUCTION

My first encounter with the SAT Writing section came in early 2006, when I answered an online advertisement for practice-SAT test writers. The exam had recently been overhauled to include the Writing section, and suddenly test-prep companies needed lots of new material fast. The first questions I wrote, I regret to say, were not particularly faithful to the actual test. I simply leafed through a College Board guide, generally noted the sorts of questions that appeared, and wrote approximations. No one complained, so I assumed I was doing fine.

As I began spending more time tutoring SAT Writing, however, I began to investigate the section more deeply. Most of my students had little to no familiarity with grammatical terminology, so rather than simply reviewing concepts and offering up a couple of tricks, I had to teach them virtually all of the fundamentals of grammar. And I had to do it fast; there simply wasn't time to teach them four years worth of grammar and then apply it all to the test. Moreover, even if students did have some knowledge of grammar, they simply couldn't figure out what the questions were asking. It seemed that anything could be wrong with those sentences.

So I went back to the College Board book and labeled the kind of error contained in every single multiple-choice grammar question. When I was done, I made a list of all the categories of questions, ranking them in order of frequency. And I began to notice things. I noticed that punctuation problems, for example, occurred only in certain places, as did dangling modifiers and certain kinds of parallelism problems.

More importantly, I noticed that certain key words or phrases included in a sentence often pointed to particular errors.

For example:

-An underlined pronoun often pointed to a pronoun error.

-An underlined verb in the present tense frequently pointed to a subject-verb agreement error.

-The presence of a comparison such as *more than/ less than* at the end of the Error-Identification section almost always pointed to a faulty comparison.

-The mention of a profession – physicist, veterinarian, or, in one memorable College Board question, entomologist (someone who studies insects) – virtually always indicated a noun agreement question.

And I had a realization: the questions themselves revealed what they were testing.

Furthermore, I noticed that specific kinds of questions always showed up at specific points in the test. For example:

-Faulty comparisons almost always showed up in the last three Error-Identification questions, as did certain kinds of tricky subject-verb agreement questions.

-The final Fixing Sentences question (#11 in the first Writing section, #14 in the second) very frequently dealt with parallel structure.

And so on.

I had cracked the test.

When I started teaching my students to actually anticipate the errors they would find on the test, their scores skyrocketed. The first student I worked with this way raised her SAT Writing score a whopping 180 points to a 750; the next one raised his by 190 points to a 700. Both were admitted to top schools. Although their Writing scores were hardly the deciding factors – both were straight-A students – it is unlikely that either of their applications would have gotten nearly as close a look with Writing scores in the 500s.

When I was working with both of these students, however, I had a finite number of College Board tests to tutor from. Afraid that I would run out of material, I went to the bookstore and looked through the standard commercially-produced test-prep books for additional exercises. When I looked closely at the practice questions they provided, I realized that not only did they frequently omit a number of major kinds of errors that regularly occurred on the exam, but they also covered rules that were never even tested! Furthermore, the level of the language contained in the sentences was often significantly easier than that found on the actual test. And the correct answer choices often seemed thoroughly arbitrary, a situation that is not true of the SAT. Even if there are "trick" answers, the right answer is the right answer because it conforms to a particular grammatical rule (not, incidentally, invented by the College Board). So I started writing my own questions. What started as ten or fifteen sentences jotted down on a piece of scrap paper gradually multiplied and multiplied and eventually became this book.

This guide is designed to systematically cover every major concept and type of question that can be reasonably expected to occur on the multiple-choice component of the SAT Writing section. Through a series of cumulative exercises, it also aims to continually reinforce concepts so that material covered early on will not be forgotten. While it contains information that applies to situations well beyond the SAT, its primary focus is that test, and my aim throughout is to make clear the application of particular grammatical rules to the precise ways in which the College Board handles them. I have therefore deliberately simplified explanations of some grammatical principles in order to make certain concepts easier to grasp, and I have also avoided including information that does not directly relate to the exam. The SAT will usually include a few unpredictable questions, but in general, 95% or so of the material tested can be safely anticipated. The goal of this book is to teach you how to anticipate it.

Erica Meltzer
New York City
July 2011

Multiple-Choice Grammar: Overview

The SAT contains 49 multiple-choice grammar and style questions divided between two Writing sections. Those two sections are always arranged as follows:

First Section: 35 questions

-11 Fixing Sentences
-18 Error-Identification
-6 Fixing Paragraphs

Second Section: 14 questions

-14 Fixing Sentences
-Always Section 10

The three kinds of multiple-choice Writing questions are as follows:

1) Fixing Sentences: 25 questions

Test-takers are presented with a sentence, a portion of which is underlined, and are asked to choose the best version.

2) Error-Identification: 18 questions

Test-takers are presented with a sentence that has four underlined words or phrases, along with a "No error" option (always choice E), and must identify which part, if any, contains an error.

3) Fixing Paragraphs: 6 questions

Test-takers are presented with a short paragraph and are asked questions covering organization, grammar, and logical arrangement of information. Since it is necessary to identify the main idea of the paragraph and decide which evidence best supports it, this section combines both reading and writing skills.

In principle, Error-Identification and Fixing Sentences questions are intended to run from least to most difficult. So, for example, in the first Writing section, #11 is the most difficult Fixing Sentences question, but #12, the first Error-Identification question, starts over at the easiest level. Fixing Paragraphs questions are distributed in no particular order of difficulty.

In addition, a given letter is frequently used as the correct answer three times consecutively, so test-takers' attempts to outsmart the test by avoiding the letter they chose for the previous question are almost always unsuccessful.

Because the multiple-choice Writing section contains fewer questions than either Math or Critical Reading, students often wonder what all the fuss is about. After all, why memorize dozens of error-identification rules when there are only 18 questions on the entire test? The answer is that because there are fewer questions, each one counts a lot more. Consider this: the difference between a 700 and an 800 on the multiple-choice is about four questions. In contrast, it's possible to miss up to three, or skip up to four, Critical Reading questions on some tests and still get an 800. But if you want a 750+ – or even a 700 – on Writing, you basically have to get everything right.

A Note About Content

SAT Writing questions cover standard concepts of grammar and usage that high school juniors can reasonably be expected to have encountered. There is a heavy emphasis on subject-verb and pronoun agreement issues, as well as on parallel structure. Test-takers are expected to be able to differentiate between sentences and fragments and to select the version of a sentence that is clearest and most logical – all skills that are necessary for good analytical (not creative!) writing.

One of the most important features of SAT grammar questions, however, is the utter predictability of both their content and their structure. Specific concepts are *always* tested in specific ways, with some concepts appearing only in Fixing Sentences and others only in Error-Identification. Furthermore, although the sentences may seem random, their structures as well as the underlined words and phrases they contain frequently indicate the rules they are testing. That is, if you know what to look for.

Let me reiterate: the sentences that you will encounter on the SAT are not random assortments of confusing words. They are deliberate constructions, carefully arranged to test specific skills. All of things you can get away with when you write papers – the unnecessary commas, the semicolons that you're not 100% certain about, the arbitrary use of *which* and *that* – are fair game on the SAT. In fact, the test specifically targets those concepts, and if you don't know a rule, there's absolutely no way to fudge it and hope the Scantron scoring your test just doesn't notice.

So if you look at a sentence and think, "That sounds funny," you're probably thinking exactly what the College Board wants you to think. The sentence has been designed to sound that way precisely because most other high school students will think so as well. Keep in mind that the College Board tests all of its questions before it includes them on actual exams. That's what the experimental section is for.

Now, your ear could be right – and if you've read non-stop for the last ten years and have been exposed to a wide variety of English prose, it very well might be – but for most test-takers, it could just as well be wrong. Assuming that most people answer the questions by ear, the College Board has arranged the exam so that the average high school junior or senior will get most of the easy questions right, some of the medium questions right, and most of the hard questions wrong. So if you want a really high score, you're better off knowing the actual rules being tested. Cold.

When I first started picking apart exams and grouping their questions by category, I did not quite understand why the College Board chose to focus so heavily on certain types of errors (subject-verb agreement, pronoun agreement, parallel structure) and virtually ignore others. Contrary to what most guides say, "who vs. whom" is not actually tested on the SAT, even though *who*, and very occasionally *whom*, are underlined on various questions. Then, as a tutor, I read the writing of high school students – lots of them. And I started to notice that most of their writing was full of the exact errors tested on the SAT. Here it seems that the College Board does actually know what it's doing.

In my experience, most high school students will often pick wordier and more awkward constructions ("Being as it rained, I decided to stay home.") rather than simple and clear ones ("Because it rained, I decided to stay home.") if given the opportunity to do so because they mistakenly believe that the wordier ones sound more sophisticated. (Hint: they don't). The SAT favors clarity and simplicity, good goals for most high school students to aim for in their analytical writing.

From what I have observed, students who devote a reasonable amount of time to studying SAT grammar will often begin to notice and spontaneously correct errors both in their own and in other people's writing. I have had students email me, genuinely thrilled to have spotted a dangling modifier in a magazine or on a website.

I often tell my students that if they learn the rules and then decide to ignore them, it's their right; but that if they are going to break the rules, they should do so deliberately and in order to create a particular stylistic effect, not because they don't know how to write correctly. It's the difference between being in control of your writing – being able to express your thoughts clearly and coherently – and being at its mercy. And it's a big difference.

Parts of Speech

There are eight parts of speech in the English language, seven of which are tested on the SAT. If you are not comfortable identifying them, it is suggested that you begin by reviewing this section. Although portions of these definitions are repeated throughout the guide, familiarizing yourself with these terms before you begin will help you move through the explanations and exercises more easily. Even if you are already comfortable identifying parts of speech, it is strongly suggested that you complete the exercise beginning on page 8.

The seven major parts of speech tested on the SAT are as follows:

1. Verb

Verbs indicate **actions** or **states of being**.

Examples: To be
To have
To seem
To go
To speak
To believe

The "to" form of a verb is known as the **infinitive**. All of the verbs listed above are infinitives. If you are uncertain whether a word can be used as a verb, try placing *to* in front of it to form an infinitive.

Verbs are not always used as infinitives, however. In order to indicate who is performing an action, we must **conjugate** the verb and provide its **subject**.

To be and *to have* are the most frequently tested verbs on the SAT. Because they are **irregular**, their conjugated forms are different from their infinitives; you must therefore make sure that you are comfortable distinguishing between their singular and plural forms.

Conjugation of the verb *to be:*

Singular	**Plural**
I am	We are
You are	You (pl.) are
He, She, It, One is	They are

Conjugation of the verb *to have:*

Singular	**Plural**
I have	We have
You have	You (pl.) have
He, She, It, One has	They have

The **number** of a verb tells us whether it is singular or plural.

I, you, he, she, it, one speaks = Singular

We, you, they speak = Plural

The **tense** of a verb tells us when an action occurred.

She speaks = Present	She would speak = Conditional
She has spoken = Present Perfect	She would have spoken = Past Conditional
She spoke = Simple Past	She will speak = Future
She had spoken = Past Perfect	She will have spoken = Future Perfect

2. Noun

Nouns indicate people, places, objects, and ideas, and can always be preceded by *a(n)* or *the*. **Proper nouns** indicate specific people and places.

> **Examples:** house, bicycle, supervisor, notion, Mark Twain, Chicago
>
> The **girl** rode her **bicycle** down the **street** to her **house**.
>
> The **politician** walked out of the **press conference** in **Washington** with his **head** in his **hands**.

3. Pronoun

Pronouns replace nouns.

> **Examples:** she, you, one, we, him, it(s), their, this, that, which, both, some, few, many, (n)either
>
> Samantha loves basketball. **She** plays **it** every day after school.
>
> Marco walks to school with Sherri and Ann. **He** meets **them** at the corner.

Personal Pronouns are often referred to in the following manner:

1st Person Singular = I	1st Person Plural = We
2nd Person Singular = You	2nd Person Plural = You
3rd Person Singular = He, She, It, One	3rd Person Plural = They

4. Preposition

Prepositions indicate where someone/something is, or when something happened.

> **Example:** The dog ran **under** <u>the fence</u> and jumped **into** <u>the neighboring yard</u>
> **in** only a <u>matter</u> **of** <u>seconds</u>.

Common prepositions include:

Of	To	Within/out	Over	Beside	Next to	Against
From	At	Above	Above	About	Toward(s)	Upon
In	For	Under	Along	Among	Before	Around
On	By	Beneath	Beyond	Near	After	Outside
Off	With	Below	Behind	Across	During	Opposite

5. Adjective

Adjectives modify nouns and pronouns.

> **Examples:** large, pretty, interesting, solid, wide, exceptional, smart, dull, caring, simple
>
> The class was so **boring** that I thought I would fall asleep.
>
> The **stunning** view left him at a loss for words.
>
> It was so **exciting** I could hardly contain myself.

6. Adverb

Adverbs modify verbs, adjectives, and other adverbs. They frequently end in –ly

> **Examples:** rapidly, calmly, serenely, shockingly, mildly, boldly, sharply, well, fast, very
>
> She smiled **warmly** at him when he entered the room.
>
> He received an **exceedingly** good grade on the test.

7. Conjunction

Conjunctions indicate relationships between words, phrases, and clauses.

> **Examples:** and, but, however, therefore, so, although, yet, when
>
> Alice went to the dentist, **but** first she went to the candy store.
>
> **Although** it has been raining all week, it should be sunny tomorrow.

Preliminary Exercise: Identifying Parts of Speech

For the following sentences, identify the part of speech contained in each underlined word or phrase. (Answers p. 157)

[handwritten: Adj   noun   Verb   Prep]

1. A large stash of books that once belonged to Thomas Jefferson was recently
   A   B   C   D   E

   discovered.

[handwritten: Conjunction   Adj   Pronoun]

2. Although the center of Los Angeles has long been famous for its traffic jams,
   A   B   C

   [handwritten: Adverb   Prep]

   the city's center is becoming increasingly accessible to pedestrians.
                                  D   E

[handwritten: Prep   Verb   Adverb]

3. The presence of the Olympic stadium has transformed the formerly run-down
       A   B   C

   [handwritten: noun]

   area of the city.
        D   E

[handwritten: Adverb   Cons Prep / Pro]

4. The author's first novel has received generally favorable reviews, but it has thus
                                          A   B   C

   [handwritten: Verb   Adj Verb]

   far failed to become an overwhelming success.
              D   E

[handwritten: Verb   prep Preposition   verb]

5. The increasing emphasis on test scores has some education experts concerned
       A   B   C

   [handwritten: verb   verb]

   that young children's ability to learn through play is being compromised.
                                 D   E

[handwritten: noun Verb   Verb   Verb]

6. The discovery that both Lewis Carroll and Chopin had epilepsy is threatening to
       A   B   C

   [handwritten: noun]

   redefine the concept of genius.
                D   E

[handwritten: Adj]

7. Drum languages, once common throughout Africa as a means of sending
                        A   B

   [handwritten: verb   Pro verb]

   messages, began to disappear almost as soon as they were documented.
             C   D   E

8

8. <u>British</u> scientist J.D. Bernal <u>believed</u> that people would <u>eventually</u> be replaced

   A   B   C

<u>by</u> creatures that <u>were</u> half-human and half-machine.

  D   E

9. New research <u>shows</u> that <u>those</u> <u>who</u> live on islands are far more likely to

                  A   B   C

suffer <u>from</u> obesity than those who live in other <u>environments</u>.

       D   E

10. The <u>book</u> *Cane*, written <u>by</u> poet and author Jean Toomer, <u>contains</u> a mix <u>of</u>

        A   B   C   D

    fiction, poetry, and <u>drama</u>.

                           E

11. Protests <u>against</u> the country's government <u>have</u> been growing in

                A   B

recent days, and observers <u>fear</u> that they may <u>explode</u> into utter chaos.

  C   D   E

12. Painted by Paul Cézanne, *The Card Players* <u>depicts</u> three men seated <u>around</u>

                                                  A   B

a table, <u>with</u> a fourth gazing <u>watchfully</u> <u>in</u> the background.

        C   D   E

13. <u>It</u> is arguable whether Mark Augustus Landis, responsible <u>for</u> perpetrating

   A

one <u>of</u> the <u>largest</u> art-forgery sprees ever, ever actually <u>broke</u> the law.

    C   D   E

14. <u>Activities</u> such as bird-watching <u>evolved</u> from people's desire to observe the

     A   B

<u>natural</u> world without <u>actively</u> participating in <u>it</u>.

   C   D   E

15. <u>Australian</u> geography is <u>remarkably</u> varied; although Australia <u>is</u> the world's

     A   B   C

<u>smallest</u> continent, <u>it</u> is the sixth largest country.

   D   E

Error-Identification: Introduction

Error-Identification questions fall into 16 major categories, listed below in approximate descending order of frequency. Please note that errors involving verbs and pronouns appear far more often than any other kind of error and comprise approximately one-third of the multiple choice grammar questions.

Verbs:

1. Subject-Verb Agreement
2. Verb Tense/Form

Pronouns:

3. Pronoun-Antecedent
4. Pronoun Case

Additional Errors:

5. Adjectives vs. Adverbs
6. Parallel Structure: Lists
7. Prepositions/Idioms
8. Faulty Comparisons
9. Word Pairs
10. Noun Agreement
11. Comparatives vs. Superlatives
12. Relative Pronouns
13. Double Negatives/Double Positives
14. Conjunctions
15. Redundancy
16. Diction

While other kinds of errors such as misplaced modifiers or conjunctions do appear in Error-Identification, they are comparatively rare, and I have thus chosen to discuss them in the section devoted to Fixing Sentences.

The format of Error-Identification questions is deceptively simple: a sentence is presented with four options underlined (corresponding to choices A, B, C, and D), along with a "No error" option (E), and the test-taker is asked to identify which choice, if any, contains an error. There are, however, two potential difficulties:

1) Several of the underlined words or phrases often sound as if they could be wrong.

Typically, the more test-takers contemplate the choices, the more they start to think that, well, it could be just about any of the answers.

That's why I've nicknamed this section, "Is it weird, or is it wrong?" Sometimes it can just be very hard to tell.

2) Option E

Option E (aka the dreaded "No error" option) is the bane of most students' existence on this section. They want there to be an error so badly.... It just seems wrong for there not to be one – the section is called "Identifying Sentence *Errors*," after all! – and the sentence sounds so awkward. Besides, ETS wouldn't ever be cruel enough to do it twice in a row.

In fact, it isn't that cruel. It's crueler. ETS has actually been known to make the answer E three times in a row. Hey, get over it. The test-writers can do whatever they want.

The most important thing to keep in mind is that finding the right answer often has nothing to do with figuring how you would say the sentence. Again, this does work sometimes, but unless your ear is always spot on, you're likely to end up with a score somewhere in the 500s. Remember, the test is designed that way. It isn't uncommon for test-takers to get hung up on a tiny little unfamiliar turn of phrase while missing a massive grammatical error staring them right in the face. If, on the other hand, you train yourself to know exactly – and I mean exactly – what to look for, the errors will virtually pop out at you. But that takes practice.

So let's go.

1. VERBS

Two types of verb questions appear on the SAT:

1) Subject-Verb Agreement

2) Verb Tense and Form

Subject-Verb Agreement

All verbs must agree with their subject in number:

-Singular subjects take singular verbs.
-Plural subjects take plural verbs.

Virtually all SAT questions that deal with number ask about verbs in the 3rd person singular (*he/she/it/one*) and 3rd person plural (*they*) forms.

3rd person singular verbs always end with an –s; 3rd person plural verbs do not. Note that this is the opposite of nouns, which take an –s in the plural rather than the singular.

	Correct	**Incorrect**
Singular Subject:	The politician speaks.	The politician speak.
Plural Subject:	The politicians speak.	The politicians speaks.
	The politician and her aide are holding a press conference.	The politician and her aide is holding a press conference.

Unfortunately, most subject-verb agreement questions that appear on the SAT are not nearly this straightforward. Subjects rarely appear next to the their verbs, making it difficult to spot disagreements.

The ways in which the SAT separates subjects from their verbs are, however, highly predictable. It is important that you practice recognizing the following structures because they will appear over and over again.

Important: *is/are*, *was/were*, and *has/have* are the most frequently tested verbs; when you see one of them underlined, you should begin by checking its subject.

Also: In the vast majority of questions in which subject-verb disagreements occur, the verb rather than the subject will be underlined. On exceedingly rare occasions, though, the subject may be underlined. It is therefore technically possible for a sentence to contain a subject-verb agreement error even if no verb is underlined. You will not, however, find both the subject and the verb underlined.

A. Subject – Non-Essential Clause – Verb

Identifying Non-Essential Clauses

A **non-essential clause** describes a noun, often (but not always) the noun that is the subject of a sentence. It is known as a non-essential clause because the description or information it provides is not essential to the meaning of the sentence – it's more like an interruption, which means it can be removed without causing any major grammatical problem or change in meaning. Non-essential clauses have two main identifying features:

1) They are surrounded by commas.

2) If they are removed from a sentence, the sentence will still make perfect grammatical sense.

In addition:

-They often begin with a "w-word" (or **relative pronoun**), such as *which, who, whose,* and *where,* that refers to the noun immediately preceding it.

-They are usually followed by verbs.

Let us examine the following sentence:

> Moroccan green tea, **which is prepared with a healthy dose of sugar and mint leaves,** is one of the most popular drinks across North Africa.

When we examine the sentence's structure, we see it contains a **relative clause** that begins with *which* and that is surrounded by commas. If we remove that clause, we are left with:

> Moroccan green tea […] is one of the most popular drinks across North Africa.

The sentence that remains makes complete sense on its own.

Appositives

It is not absolutely necessary to begin a non-essential clause with a "w-word," however. A non-essential clause that does not begin with one of those words is known as an **appositive.** You do not have to remember the term, but you do have to be able to recognize that the structure is correct, even though it may sound odd to you. For example:

> Correct: Moroccan green tea, **a drink prepared with a healthy amount of sugar and mint leaves,**
> is one of the most popular drinks across North Africa.

Non-Essential Clauses on the SAT

On the SAT, non-essential clauses are typically inserted between subjects and verbs in order to distract the test-taker from the fact that the subject is singular and the verb is plural or vice-versa.

> Incorrect: <u>Moroccan green tea</u>, which is prepared with a healthy amount of sugar and mint leaves, **are** one of the most popular drinks across North Africa.

> Correct: <u>Moroccan green tea</u>, which is prepared with a healthy amount of sugar and mint leaves, **is** one of the most popular drinks across North Africa.

Whenever you encounter a non-essential clause, you should immediately cross it out. Most often it is used to distract you from spotting subject-verb agreement errors, but it can be used to distract from other types of errors as well (described later). Do not forget to do this! Otherwise, you risk overlooking errors that can be easily spotted.

Sometimes, however, the error will appear *within* the non-essential clause, so if you've crossed one out and can't find another problem in the sentence, go back and check. For example:

Incorrect: <u>Moroccan green tea</u>, which **are** prepared with a healthy amount of sugar and mint leaves, is one of the most popular drinks across North Africa.

Correct: <u>Moroccan green tea</u>, which **is** prepared with a healthy amount of sugar and mint leaves, is one of the most popular drinks across North Africa.

Occasionally, you will encounter a non-essential clause followed by the word *and*. This construction is always wrong because if you cross out the non-essential clause, you are left with nonsense:

Incorrect: <u>Moroccan green tea</u>, which is prepared with a healthy amount of sugar and mint leaves, **and it is** one of the most popular drinks across North Africa.

Incorrect: Moroccan green tea and it is one of the most popular drinks across North Africa.

Essential Clauses with "That"

Occasionally, you will see subject-verb agreement questions based on **essential clauses** beginning with *that*. Such clauses are not set off by commas, but the verbs they contain must still agree with their subjects.

Incorrect: Green tea is a beverage <u>that</u> **have** long been used as a form of medicine in many countries.

Correct: Green tea is a beverage <u>that</u> **has** long been used as a form of medicine in many countries.

B. Subject – Prepositional Phrase – Verb

A prepositional phrase is, quite simply, a phrase that begins with a preposition (e.g. *in the box*, *under the table*, *over the hill*). These are often inserted between subjects and verbs to distract from disagreements.

In the sentences below, the subject is underlined, the prepositional phrase is italicized, and the verb is in bold.

Incorrect: <u>Changes</u> *in the balance of trade* **seems** remote from everyday concerns, but they can drastically affect how we spend our money.

Correct: <u>Changes</u> *in the balance of trade* **seem** remote from everyday concerns, but they can drastically affect how we spend our money.

The above sentence contains a classic trick: the subject (*changes*) is plural and thus requires a plural verb (*seem*). However, the prepositional phrase inserted between the subject and the verb has as its last word a singular noun (*trade*), which, if you are not paying close attention, can easily appear to be the subject of the verb that follows. If you don't see an error the first time you read a sentence, cross out all prepositional phrases and check for subject-verb agreement.

The last word of a prepositional phrase will always be the last word right before the verb, so be careful not to cross out verbs when getting rid of prepositional phrases.

Hint: If you see an underlined verb close to the beginning of a sentence, the subject will usually be the first word or couple of words of the sentence.

C. Prepositional Phrase – Verb – Subject

In this structure, the normal word order (or **syntax**) of a sentence is reversed so that the prepositional phrase appears at the beginning of a sentence, followed by the verb and then subject, always in that order.

In the sentences below, the subject is underlined, the prepositional phrase is italicized, and the verb is in bold.

Incorrect: *Along the Loup Canal in Nebraska* **extends** parks, lakes, and trails owned and operated by the Loup power district.

Correct: *Along the Loup Canal in Nebraska* **extend** parks, lakes, and trails owned and operated by the Loup power district.

Prepositional Phrase–Verb–Subject errors almost always appear as questions #27-29 and are signaled by a preposition at the beginning of the sentence. Most often, the preposition will be the first word of the sentence, but sometimes it will be the second.

Incorrect: Running *along the Loup Canal in Nebraska* **is** parks, lakes, and trails owned and operated by the Loup power district.

Correct: Running *along the Loup Canal in Nebraska* **are** parks, lakes, and trails owned and operated by the Loup power district.

It is common for test-takers to become confused because the reversed syntax makes the sentence sound odd. It is important to understand, however, that the unusual syntax is not what makes the sentence incorrect. It is simply a distraction to keep you from hearing the disagreement between the subject and the verb.

Sometimes a sentence in this form will not contain an agreement error; in those cases, the answer is very likely to be "No error."

Important: the SAT will often incorrectly pair two singular nouns connected by *and* (a structure known as a **compound subject**) with a singular verb, especially in Prepositional Phrase–Verb–Subject sentences, so always make sure you determine the *entire* subject before deciding whether the verb is right or wrong.

Usual Syntax: A park and a lake **runs** *along the Loup Canal*, a hydroelectric and irrigation canal located in eastern Nebraska.

Unusual Syntax: *Along the Loup Canal* **runs** a park and a lake, both of which are owned and operated by the Loup Power District.

Note that in the second version, the error is much more difficult to hear.

It is also important that you determine the entire subject because errors will very occasionally appear in which the verb comes before the subject but is not preceded by a prepositional phrase:

Incorrect: Radioactivity is generally not considered harmful when people are exposed to it at low levels for brief periods, but less clear **is** its long-term effects.

Correct: Radioactivity is generally not considered harmful when people are exposed to it at low levels for brief periods, but less clear **are** its long-term effects.

D. There is/There are, etc.

There is
There was
There has been
} go with **singular** nouns

There are
There were
There have been
} go with **plural** nouns

Incorrect: In recent months, there **has been** <u>many questions</u> raised about the handling of the company's finances.

Correct: In recent months, there **have been** <u>many questions</u> raised about the handling of the company's finances.

E. Neither...Nor + Verb

When *neither* and *nor* are used with two singular nouns, the verb should be singular.

Neither (Singular Noun) + Nor (Singular Noun) = Singular Verb

Incorrect: Neither the <u>senator</u> nor her <u>aide</u> **are** expected to appear at the press conference today.

Correct: Neither the <u>senator</u> nor her <u>aide</u> **is** expected to appear at the press conference today.

Although rule is the same for *either...or*, that word pair is not generally tested in regard to subject-verb agreement.

In general, the SAT only incorrectly pairs singular nouns connected by *neither...nor* with plural verbs. It is **highly unlikely** that an error involving plural nouns, or combined singular and plural nouns, would appear.

The rule, however, is that the verb must take the number of the noun that follows *nor* (e.g. "Neither the senator nor <u>her aide</u> **is** expected to speak to the press today," BUT: "Neither the senator nor <u>her aides</u> **are** expected to speak to the press today").

When *(n)either* is not paired with *(n)or* and is used with two singular nouns, a singular verb should also be used:

Incorrect: Both the senator and her aide appeared at the press conference, but neither **were** willing to speak to reporters.

Correct: Both the senator and her aide appeared at the press the conference, but neither **was** willing to speak to reporters.

Very Important:

Collective Nouns = Singular

Collective Nouns are **singular nouns** that refer to groups of people. Common examples include *agency, institution, school, committee, jury, city, country, company, university,* and *team*. While many people consider it perfectly acceptable to use such nouns with plural verbs, the SAT only considers **singular** verbs to be correct.

Incorrect:	After many days of deliberation, <u>the jury</u> **have** finally returned with a verdict.
Correct:	After many days of deliberation, <u>the jury</u> **has** finally returned with a verdict.

Watch out for collective nouns. They appear often, and their presence in a sentence often indicates an agreement error.

A number of = Plural

The number = Singular

Correct:	<u>A number of</u> workers **are** beginning to protest the economic policies instituted by the new administration.
BUT	
Correct:	<u>The number</u> of workers beginning to protest the new administration's economic policies **is** unexpectedly high.

Each = Singular

Incorrect:	<u>Each</u> of the labor union's members **are** expected to attend the meeting at which next year's contract will be negotiated with company officials.
Correct:	<u>Each</u> of the members of the labor union **is** expected to attend the meeting at which next year's contract will be negotiated with company officials.

(Every) One = Singular

Incorrect:	<u>(Every) one</u> of the labor union's members **are** expected to attend the meeting, at which next year's contract will be negotiated with company officials.
Correct:	<u>(Every) one</u> of the labor union's members **is** expected to attend the meeting, at which next year's contract will be negotiated with company officials.

Gerunds when used as subjects = Singular

Incorrect:	<u>Playing</u> parlor games such as charades **were** a popular pastime in the early twentieth century, before the invention of radio and television.
Correct:	<u>Playing</u> parlor games such as charades **was** a popular pastime in the early twentieth century, before the invention of radio and television.

Subject-Verb Agreement Exercises

In the following sentences, fix any subject-verb agreement error that appears. Label all subjects, verbs, and prepositional phrases, and make sure to cross out any non-essential clauses. Some of the sentences may not contain an error. (Answers p. 157, Official Guide question list p. 139)

1. The process of living vicariously through a fictional character in order to purge one's emotions are known as catharsis.

2. Along the border between China and Tibet lies the Himalaya Mountains, which include some of the highest peaks in the world.

3. Recognized for formulating unorthodox social theories, Lev Gumilev and D.S. Mirsky was *were* partly responsible for founding the neo-eurasianist political and cultural movement.

4. The works of artist Alan Chin draws *draw* inspiration from both the California gold rush and the construction of the transcontinental railroad.

5. The maps of historian and cartographer John Speed depict some of the first visual representations of many towns and cities throughout England, Ireland, and Scotland.

6. Playboating, a discipline of whitewater rafting or canoeing in which players stay in one spot while performing certain maneuvers, involves specialized canoes designed for the sport.

7. Often found in plastic drinking bottles is *are* substantial amounts of a potentially toxic chemical called Bisphenol A.

8. The African violet, which is known for its striking pink and purple leaves, belong to the Saintpaulia family of flowering plants rather than to the violet family.

9. Among the finds from a recent archaeological dig in London was *were* earthenware knobs originally used for "pay walls," boxes into which Elizabethan theater-goers deposited their admission fees.

10. One of the animal kingdom's best jumpers is the flea, whose ability to leap up to 200 times its own body length is nearly unsurpassed.

11. Stiles, structures that provides people with a passage through or over a fence, are often built in rural areas or along footpaths.

12. The patent for the first mechanical pencils were *was* granted to Sampson Morgan and John Hawkins in England during the early nineteenth century.

13. Each of the Taino's five chiefdoms, which inhabited the Bahamas before the arrival of Europeans, were *was* ruled by a leader known as a cacique.

14. If there is *are* sufficient funds remaining, the teacher's request for new classroom supplies will most likely be approved by the school board.

15. Possible explanations for the suspicion surrounding Shakespeare's *Macbeth* includes the superstition that the witches' song is an actual incantation and the belief that theaters only mount the play when they are in need of money.

16. In the galleries of the Louvre museum hang *correct* Leonardo da Vinci's *Mona Lisa* and Eugene Delacroix's *Liberty Leading the People*, two of the best-known paintings in the world.

17. Galaxies, far from being randomly scattered throughout the universe, appears to be distributed in bubble-shaped patterns.

18. For the past several years, the theater company *was* ~~have~~ traveled to various schools throughout the city in order to expose students to classic works.

19. Over the past several days, a number of disturbing reports *have* ~~has~~ filtered in to the news agency, suggesting that the country's government is on the verge of collapse.

20. According to the law of diminution, the pitches of notes sounded by an orchestra remains the same even as the amount of sound diminishes.

21. There are a number of prominent economists who consider changes in the demand for goods to be one of the fundamental causes of inflation.

22. Although the criminal protested his innocence vehemently, neither he nor his lawyer *was* ~~were~~ ultimately able to offer a convincing alibi.

23. Sebastian Díaz Morales, like the other members of his generation of artists, *knew* ~~knows~~ how to draw on the social experiences of his country to produce works that entirely escape any simple interpretation.

24. Historians describe the chariot as a simple type of horse carriage that *was* ~~were~~ used by ancient civilizations for peacetime travel and military combat.

25. Along the deepest part of the ocean floor sits the Mariana Trench and the HMRG Deep, the two lowest spots that researchers have ever identified on earth.

Verb Tense and Form

Like subject-verb agreement errors, verb tense and form errors regularly appear on the SAT in specific formats and in highly predictable ways.

The inclusion of a date or time period in a sentence is usually a tip-off that the question is testing verb tense. When you see one of these clues, make sure to check the tenses of all verbs <u>first</u>.

A. Consistency

Verbs should remain consistent (or **parallel**) in tense or form throughout a sentence.

Unless the information in the sentence clearly indicates otherwise, sentences that start in the past should stay in the past, and sentences that start in the present should stay in the present.

Incorrect:	Since serious drama unaccompanied by music **was** forbidden in all but two London theatres during the eighteenth century, the renowned Queen's Theatre **becomes** an opera house.
Correct:	Since serious drama unaccompanied by music **was** forbidden in all but two London theatres during the eighteenth century, the renowned Queen's Theatre **became** an opera house.

The sentence begins in the past tense, as indicated by the verb *was*, and must continue in the past tense since there is nothing to suggest otherwise.

B. Date in the Past = Simple Past

Any sentence that includes a date or time period in the past and that describes a completed action should contain a verb in the **simple past (**e.g. *he went, she drank*) only. Often, the **present perfect** (e.g. *he has gone, she has drunk*) will be incorrectly used instead.

Incorrect:	During the <u>nineteenth century</u>, Charles Dickens **has been renowned** as one of the most famous British novelists.
Correct:	During the <u>nineteenth century</u>, Charles Dickens **was renowned** as one of the most famous British novelists.

In the above sentence, the time period "nineteenth century" indicates that the verb must be in the simple past.

C. Would vs. Will

Would and *Will* are switched almost exclusively with one another.

Whenever you see *would* or *will* underlined in a sentence, replace it with the other one and see if it works better.

If you are unsure when to use *would* vs. *will*, the rule is that you should not mix past and future in the same sentence, unless there is an extremely clear reason for doing so.

-Sentences that contain verbs in the past tense should not contain the word *will*.

-Sentences that contain verbs in the present tense should not contain the word *would*.

Incorrect:	William Shakespeare, who **will** become the greatest English dramatist, **was** born in Stratford-upon-Avon in 1564.
Correct:	William Shakespeare, who **would** become the greatest English dramatist, **was** born in Stratford-upon-Avon in 1564.

In the incorrect version of the above sentence, for example, the verb *was* appears. Since *was* is a verb in the past tense, *will become*, a verb in the future tense, should not also appear. And since *will* and *would* are switched with one another, *would become* must be the correct answer.

Likewise, a sentence containing a verb in the present tense should not contain *would*.

Incorrect:	If union members and company officials reach a compromise today, a labor crisis **would** most likely be averted.
Correct:	If union members and company officials reach a compromise today, a labor crisis **will** most likely be averted.

Since the verb *reach* is in the present tense, *would* cannot be correct. *Will* is the only other option.

Important: although a sentence can contain both *would have* and *if*, the two should not appear together in the same clause. *Had* should be used in place of *would have*. (For more information, see p. 124.)

Incorrect:	If company officials and union leaders **would have compromised** on several important issues today, the labor crisis would have been averted.
Correct:	If company officials and union leaders **had compromised** on several important issues today, the labor crisis would have been averted.

D. Gerunds vs. Infinitives

Infinitive = TO form of a verb

Gerund = -ING form of a verb*

Infinitive	Gerund
To be	Being
To have	Having
To go	Going

On the SAT, gerunds and infinitives are nearly always switched with one another. If you see a gerund underlined, plug in the infinitive and vice-versa.

Incorrect:	Though she was one of the few women of her time **gaining** international prominence, Clara Barton would not have described herself as a proponent of women's rights.
Correct:	Though she was one of the few women of her time **to gain** international prominence, Clara Barton would not have described herself as a proponent of women's rights.

---

* A gerund is a verb that acts as a noun (e.g. *I was annoyed by his singing*). When a verb acts as an adjective (e.g. *a singing bird*), it is a **participle**. Although both end in "–ing," they have different functions. For more information, see Chapter 20 on p. 110.

Important: Often, when switching a gerund with an infinitive, you must place a preposition before the gerund in order for a sentence to make sense. Inserting only the gerund will not usually fix the sentence.

Incorrect:	Deactivated viruses form the basis of many vaccines known for their effectiveness **to prevent** disease.
Incorrect:	Deactivated viruses form the basis of many vaccines known for their effectiveness **preventing** disease.
Correct:	Deactivated viruses form the basis of many vaccines known for their effectiveness **in preventing** disease.

Sometimes, both a gerund and an infinitive are acceptable. In such cases, neither will be considered incorrect.

Correct:	Today, the members of Ms. Moreno's physics class will begin **to review** for the final exam.
Correct:	Today, the members of Ms. Moreno's physics class will begin **reviewing** for the final exam.

In general, it is necessary to rely on your ear in order to determine whether the gerund or the infinitive is correct. There is no rule that governs which one is used, and the gerunds and infinitives tested are fairly random. So while I do not advocate trying to memorize all the expressions that require gerunds vs. infinitives (expressions that in all likelihood will not appear on the test), it may be helpful to know the following expressions, some which have appeared on past exams:

Idioms with Gerund	**Idioms with Infinitive**
Regarded as (being)	Consider to be
Viewed as (being)	Require to be
Seen as (being)	Deserve to be
Praised/celebrated as (being)	Agree to be
In the hope(s) of being	Promise to be
Effective in/at being	Refuse to be
Accustomed/used to being	Threaten to be
Enjoy being	Inclined to be
Admired for being	Decline to be
Capable of being	Seek/strive to be
Succeed in/at being	Encourage to be
Stop being	Choose/decide to be
Insist on being	Intend to be
Accused of being	Inspire to be
Deny being	Shown to be
Report being	Claim to be
Consider being	Arrange to be
Postpone being	Prepare to be
Avoid being	Neglect to be
Admit to being	Offer to be
Resent being	Attempt to be
Imagine being	Fail to be
Describe being	Struggle to be
Prevent from being	Want/wish to be
Without being	Reluctant to be
Mind being	Tend to be
Discuss being	Allow to be
Before being	Manage to be
After being	Appear/seem to be
Risk being	Expect to be
Banned from being	Have the ability to be
In charge of being	

E. Past Participle vs. Simple Past

The **past participle** is used after any form of the verb *to have* (e.g. *to have, had, has, having*).

Examples: **Having sung** for hours, the bird fell silent.

Since a number of unexpected issues **had arisen** during the meeting, we were forced to remain an extra hour.

Since it first opened in 1857, New York City residents **have chosen** to spend their free time relaxing in Central Park.

The verb tense that is formed by combining *have* or *has* + past participle (e.g. *has been, has gone, has chosen*) is the **present perfect**.

The present perfect is used for an action that started in the past and that is continuing into the present. When the words *for* or *since*, or a phrase such as *over the past several years*, appear, the present perfect is usually required.

Incorrect: Many groundbreaking scientific discoveries **were** made <u>since</u> the start of the twentieth century.

Correct: Many groundbreaking scientific discoveries **have been** made <u>since</u> the start of the twentieth century.

Correct: Groundbreaking scientific discoveries **have been** continually made <u>for</u> the last hundred years.

However, the **simple past** is used for actions that began and ended in the past.

The bird **sang** for hours and then fell silent.

A number of unexpected issues **arose** during the meeting, so we **were** forced to remain an extra hour.

Between 1858 and 1873, New York City's Central Park **was** improved and expanded according to a plan designed by Frederick Law Olmsted and Calvert Vaux.

On the SAT, the simple past rather than the past participle will always incorrectly follow a form of the verb *to have* or *to be*; the past participle is never used to replace the simple past (e.g. *He done the work*).

Incorrect: Having **saw** the thief sneak into her neighbor's home, the woman promptly called the police.

Correct: Having **seen** the thief sneak into her neighbor's home, the woman promptly called the police.

Many common verbs take different past participle and simple past forms, and often, if you're not paying attention, you can easily overlook errors involving them. The verb *to go*, for example, has two different forms in the past: *gone* (past participle) and *went* (simple past). Here is a list of some common verbs that have different forms for their simple past and past participle.

Infinitive	Simple Past	Past Participle
To (a)rise	(A)rose	(A)risen
To (a)waken	(A)woke	(A)woken
To be	Was	Been
To become	Became	Become
To begin	Began	Begun
To blow	Blew	Blown
To break	Broke	Broken
To choose	Chose	Chosen
To do	Did	Done
To draw	Drew	Drawn
To drink	Drank	Drunk
To drive	Drove	Driven
To fly	Flew	Flown
To freeze	Froze	Frozen
To get	Got	Gotten*
To go	Went	Gone
To hide	Hid	Hidden
To give	Gave	Given
To grow	Grew	Grown
To know	Knew	Known
To ride	Rode	Ridden
To ring	Rang	Rung
To run	Ran	Run
To see	Saw	Seen
To sew	Sewed	Sewn
To shrink	Shrank	Shrunk/Shrunken
To sink	Sank	Sunk/Sunken
To sing	Sang	Sung
To speak	Spoke	Spoken
To spring	Sprang	Sprung
To steal	Stole	Stolen
To stink	Stank	Stunk
To swim	Swam	Swum
To take	Took	Taken
To tear	Tore	Torn
To throw	Threw	Thrown
To wear	Wore	Worn
To write	Wrote	Written

---

*Although *got* is used as the past participle of *get* in British English, *gotten* is considered standard in American English.

F. The Past Perfect

Past Perfect = *Had* + Past Participle

    Examples: had done, had gone, had been, had seen

Sometimes a sentence will describe two events or actions that occurred in the past. The **past perfect** can be used to refer to the action that occurred **first**.

    Incorrect: By the time the committee members made the decision to adjourn the meeting, they **made** several important decisions.

    Correct: By the time the committee members made the decision to adjourn the meeting, they **had made** several important decisions.

Logically, the committee members must have made several important decisions (action #1) before they made the decision to adjourn (action #2); therefore, the past perfect is required.

Important: the phrase *by the time* is a tip-off that the past perfect is required.

There are, however, instances when either the past perfect or the simple past is perfectly acceptable. For example:

    Correct: Before a complete version of Louisa May Alcott's novel *Little Women* appeared in 1880, the book **had been published** in two separate volumes.

    Correct: Before a complete version of Louisa May Alcott's novel *Little Women* appeared in 1880, the book **was published** in two separate volumes.

In the first sentence, the past perfect is used to emphasize the appearance of the book in two volumes before its appearance in one; however, the simple past in the second sentence is also correct because it describes two actions that took place in the past and keeps the tense of the sentence consistent.

On the SAT, you may encounter sentences that contain only the simple past but that could also be written with the past perfect, or vice-versa, as in the first example above. (For a College Board example, see question 26, p. 957 in the *Official Guide*, 2nd Edition.) **In cases in which both the simple past and past perfect are acceptable, you will never be asked to choose between them.**

Important: Verbs in the past perfect are often underlined when they are **correct**, and you are simply responsible for recognizing that they are <u>not</u> wrong. Whenever you encounter an underlined verb in the past perfect, ask yourself whether the sentence makes it clear that the event or action the verb describes clearly occurred before a second event or action. If it does, the verb is fine as it is. (For examples, see question 17, p. 894 and question 24, p. 957). The past perfect will only be considered **wrong** when it is used to refer to an action that clearly occurred **after** or **at the same time** as a second action.

Verb Exercise #1: Present Perfect, Simple Past, and Past Perfect

For each sentence, decide whether the tense of each underlined verb is correct or incorrect. If there is an error, write the correct tense. (Answers p. 158)

1. Beginning in the eleventh century, reviving economic development **has allowed** Pamplona to recover its urban life after suffering repeated Viking invasions.

   Correct   **Incorrect**   Correction: _____

2. Despite its status as a regional capital, eighteenth century Quebec City **was** essentially a small colonial outpost that maintained close ties to its rural surroundings.

   Correct   **Incorrect**   Correction: _____

3. Although the ancient Egyptians abandoned Demotic more than 1,500 years ago, taking up Coptic and eventually Arabic, the language **lived** on in words like "adobe," which entered Spanish before passing into English.

   Correct   **Incorrect**   Correction: _____

4. In 1915, the Dutch government approved the proposal for new ships to protect its holdings in the East Indies, not realizing that the request **has been** withdrawn because of the start of the First World War.

   Correct   **Incorrect**   Correction: _____

5. Abu Dhabi is full of archeological evidence indicating that civilizations, beginning with the Umm an-Nar Culture, **have been** located there since the third millennium BC.

   Correct   **Incorrect**   Correction: _____

6. By the time Pearl S. Buck was awarded the Nobel Prize for Literature in 1938, she **was** a best-selling author in the United States for nearly a decade.

   Correct   **Incorrect**   Correction: _____

7. In 1847, Maria Mitchell **became** the first American astronomer to discover a comet; remarkably, she accomplished that feat using only a two-inch telescope.

   Correct   **Incorrect**   Correction: _____

8. During the 1950s, the Detroit area emerged as a metropolitan region with the construction of an extensive freeway system that **had expanded** in ensuing decades.

   Correct   **Incorrect**   Correction: _____

9. The Arctic Council, a once-obscure body focused on issues such as monitoring Arctic animal populations, **has begun** to handle more important tasks in recent years.

   Correct   **Incorrect**   Correction: _____

10. In a discovery at least fifty years in the making, a new and bizarre dinosaur species **has been** identified in a slab of rock collected by scientists working in South Africa in the 1960s.

    Correct   **Incorrect**   Correction: _____

Verb Exercise #2: All Tenses and Forms

In the following exercises, underline the date or words that indicate a tense question, and fix any verb not in the correct tense or form. Some of the sentences may not contain an error. (Answers p. 158, Official Guide question list p. 140)

1. Built in Newcastle upon Tyne, England and launched in 1873, the *SS Dunraven* was powered by both steam and sail and was intended to travel between Britain and India.

2. In 1498, Dutch scholar Erasmus of Rotterdam moved from Paris to England, where he becomes a professor of ancient languages at Cambridge.

3. M.J. Hyland, who authored the acclaimed 2003 novel *How the Light Gets In*, is often praised to be a subtle and complex portrayer of human psychology.

4. Were an earthquake to strike, the bridge's concrete piers will sway and absorb the majority of the shock, limiting damage to areas without extra steel reinforcements.

5. According to researchers, the Antarctic ice shelf has shrank by approximately 50 gigatons of ice each year since 1992.

6. By 1900, McKim, Mead and White had become New York's largest architectural firm; today it remains among the most famous in the city's history.

7. The nearly 200-ton Mayflower was chartered by a group of British merchants and setting sail from Plymouth, England in 1620.

8. Mahatma Gandhi, who was born in India, studied law in London and in 1893 went to South Africa, where he spends twenty years opposing discriminatory legislation against Indians.

9. Accidentally discovered by Procter and Gamble researchers in 1968, the fat substitute Olestra has been shown in causing stomach upset in those who consume excessive amounts of it.

10. The country's economists speculated that thousands more jobs would have been lost if consumer demand for domestically manufactured products would have continued to decline.

11. In the sixteenth century, writer and jurist Noël du Fail has written many stories documenting rural life in France during the Renaissance.

12. Defying predictions that he will fade from the public eye, former Czech president Vaclav Havel became a film director after his retirement from office.

13. Descended from a long line of university professors, Marie Goeppert-Mayer received the majority of her training in Germany and eventually teaching at a number of universities in the United States.

14. After a 1991 attempt to overthrow Mikhail Gorbechav failed, power had shifted to Russian president Boris Yeltsin.

15. New facts, especially when they replace beliefs already in one's mind, commonly take as long as several weeks being fully accepted as true.

16. During the Renaissance, glass products made on the island of Murano could only be crafted according to traditional techniques, and local artisans were forbidden to leave and sell their creations elsewhere.

17. The illustrator often photographed multiple models for each drawing and has made his selection only when the final prints arrived in his hands.

18. Toward the end of the sixteenth century, the Iroquois League, a confederation of six Native American nations, has formed in the northeastern United States.

19. NASA scientists have decided to delay the space shuttle's launch in order to determine whether recently repaired parts would cause damage if they break off in orbit.

20. After weeks of careful scrutiny, the consumer protection agency informed the public that a number of products will be recalled because of safety concerns.

21. Even before the beginning of the twentieth century, when the electronic age was still in its infancy, the first attempts to generate sound from electricity had already begun.

22. Far from being a recluse, Goethe corresponded with the leading literary, political, and scientific figures of his day with an energy that few of his readers could ever hope to match.

23. Several dozen boats are known to have sank off of the French Frigate Shoals, part of an enormous protected zone that covers nearly 150,000 square miles in the Pacific Ocean.

24. Emperor Frederick the Great of Prussia believed that to fight a successful war was creating minimal intrusion into the lives of civilians.

25. According to cognitive scientist Daniel Willingham, one major reason more students do not enjoy school is that abstract thought is not something our brains are designed to be good at or enjoying.

26. The Empire of Mali on the west coast of Africa was founded by King Sundiata Kesa, a hero of the Mandinka people, during the Middle Ages.

27. Hardly a stranger to self-censorship, Mark Twain never hesitated to change his prose if he believed that the alterations will improve the sales of his books.

28. Some critics have argued that Dostoevsky was unique among nineteenth-century authors in that he surrendered fully to his characters and has allowed himself to write in voices other than his own.

2. PRONOUNS

Next to verbs, pronouns are the most commonly tested part of speech on the SAT. There are two kinds of pronoun questions that appear on the SAT:

1) Pronoun-Antecedent

2) Pronoun Case

Pronoun-Antecedent

A **pronoun** is a word such as *he, she, it, them, their,* or *us* that is used to replace a noun.

> In the sentence, *The ball is on the table*, the noun *ball* can be replaced by the pronoun *it*.

> Likewise, in the sentence, *Mary threw the ball*, the name *Mary* can be replaced by the pronoun *she*.

An **antecedent** is simply the word (noun, pronoun, or gerund) to which a pronoun refers. Although the prefix *–ante* means "before," an antecedent can appear either before or after the noun to which it refers. (If you find the term "antecedent" too confusing, however, you can use **referent** instead.)

All pronouns must **agree** with their antecedents. Just as singular verbs must agree with singular subjects and plural verbs must agree with plural subjects, so must singular pronouns agree with singular nouns and plural pronouns with plural nouns.

> For example, in the sentence "Katie dribbled the ball, and then **she** shot **it** at the basket," the word *ball* is the antecedent referred to by the pronoun *it*. The word *Katie* is the antecedent of the pronoun *she*.

> If we said, "Katie dribbled the ball, and then she shot **them** at the basket," there would be a disagreement between the antecedent and the pronoun because the antecedent *ball* is singular and the pronoun *them* is plural.

> Likewise, if we said, "Katie dribbled the ball, and then **they** shot it at the basket," there would also be a pronoun-antecedent disagreement because the antecedent *Katie* is singular, while the pronoun *they* is plural.

Whenever you see a pronoun underlined, you should immediately try to figure out what noun that pronoun is referring to. If the noun and the pronoun do not agree, whichever one is underlined will be incorrect. You will never find both the noun and the pronoun underlined.

A. One vs. You

One and *You* are frequently switched with one another (although they are also occasionally switched with other pronouns). They cannot be mixed and matched within a sentence but must remain consistent throughout.

You → You
One → One

Incorrect:	If **one** wants to avoid insect invasions, **you** should refrain from leaving crumbs lying on the floor.
Correct:	If **one** wants to avoid insect invasions, **one** should refrain from leaving crumbs lying on the floor.
Correct:	If **you** want to avoid insect invasions, **you** should refrain from leaving crumbs lying on the floor.

B. Singular vs. Plural

Singular nouns are referred to by singular pronouns.

Plural nouns are referred to by plural pronouns.

Sometimes different pronouns are used to refer to people and to things.

For people (e.g. actors, judges, athletes):

For Singular Nouns		For Plural Nouns
He, She	→	They
His, Her	→	Their

Incorrect:	<u>A person</u> who wishes to become an Olympic-caliber athlete must devote virtually all of **their** time to training.
Correct:	<u>A person</u> who wishes to become an Olympic-caliber athlete must devote virtually all of **his or her** time to training.
Incorrect:	<u>People</u> who wish to become Olympic-caliber athletes must devote virtually all of **his or her** time to training.
Correct:	<u>People</u> who wish to become Olympic-caliber athletes must devote virtually all of **their** time to training.

Important: the singular of *they* will always be given as the phrase *he or she* when gender is not specified.

For things (e.g. cities, books, ideas):

For Singular Nouns   For Plural Nouns

It	→	They/Them
Its	→	Their
This	→	These
That	→	Those

Incorrect: When <u>the economy</u> does poorly, **their** performance is of all-abiding interest to the public.

Correct: When <u>the economy</u> does poorly, **its** performance is of all-abiding interest to the public.

Incorrect: <u>The lights</u> began to flicker wildly, and only moments later **it** went out altogether.

Correct: <u>The lights</u> began to flicker wildly, and only moments later **they** went out altogether.

Important: When you see *it(s)* or *they/their* underlined in a sentence, check it first because there's a very good chance that it's wrong. If the antecedent does not agree with the pronoun, you've found your error.

In addition: remember to look out for collective nouns (e.g *country*, *jury*, *university*, *agency*). They are tested frequently in regard to pronoun agreement, and because they are singular, they should always be referred to by singular pronouns (*it* or *its*).

C. Ambiguous Antecedent

Sometimes it is unclear which antecedent a pronoun refers to.

Incorrect: Afraid that they would be late to the party, <u>Rosa and Caroline</u> decided to take **her** car rather than walk.

Whose car did Rosa and Caroline take? We don't know. Since we have two female names, "her" could refer to either one of them. In order to fix this sentence, we must make it clear whose car they took. We can therefore say:

Correct: <u>Rosa and Caroline</u> decided to take **Rosa's** car to the party.

Correct: <u>Rosa and Caroline</u> decided to take **Caroline's** car to the party.

(When these questions appear in Fixing Sentences, you will *not* be given the option of saying, "Rosa and Caroline took **their** car to the party.")

D. Missing Antecedent

Any pronoun that appears in a sentence must have a **clear antecedent** that is a noun, pronoun, or gerund. If a sentence includes a pronoun without an antecedent, that sentence cannot be correct, no matter how obvious its meaning may be.

Incorrect:	In some countries, extreme weather conditions have led to shortages of food, and consequently **they** must struggle to receive adequate nutrients.

Correct:	In some countries, extreme weather conditions have led to shortages of food, and consequently **their inhabitants** must struggle to receive adequate nutrients.

In the incorrect version, it is understood that the word *they* refers to the inhabitants of countries with extreme weather conditions; however, there is no noun anywhere in the sentence that explicitly says who *they* are.

Incorrect:	In the report released by the committee, **it** stated that significant budget cuts would be necessary for the following year.

In the above sentence, we do not know who or what the word *it* refers to. The writers of the report? The report itself? The sentence never tells us. There are several ways to fix this issue in order to make the antecedent clear. We can either eliminate the pronoun completely:

Correct:	The <u>report</u> released by the treasury committee **stated** that significant budget cuts would be necessary for the following year.

Or, we can make it clear what *it* refers to:

Correct:	The <u>treasury committee stated</u> in **its** report that significant budget cuts would be necessary for the following year.

Antecedents ≠ Verbs or Adjectives

Only nouns, pronouns, and gerunds can be antecedents. Any sentence that attempts to use another part of speech, such as a **verb** or an **adjective**, as an antecedent cannot be correct.

Do so = Right
Do it = Wrong

Incorrect:	Activists who defend endangered species from poaching **do it** on the grounds that such animals, once gone, are irreplaceable.

What does *it* refer to in this sentence? *Defending* endangered species. But since the gerund *defending* doesn't actually appear in the sentence (only the verb *defend*) there is no real antecedent. When no real antecedent is present, the correct phrase is *do so*:

Correct:	Activists who defend endangered species from poaching **do so** on the grounds that such animals, once gone, are irreplaceable.

Important: when *do it* is underlined, it is virtually always wrong.

*The following errors usually appear in Fixing Sentences but are discussed here for the sake of consistency.

Adjective as "Trick" Antecedent

One of the trickiest ways that antecedents are presented in incorrect form is as follows:

Incorrect: The canine <u>penchant</u> for hierarchy has its roots in wolf society, which always designated **its** specific role within the pack.

What does *its* refer to? A canine. But *canine* isn't acting as a noun – it's actually an adjective that modifies *penchant*. And since antecedents can only be nouns or gerunds, *its* has no antecedent. What makes this so incredibly tricky is that the word *canine* is usually used as a noun – except that here it isn't. In order to make the sentence correct, we must repeat the word *canine*, this time using it as a noun.

Correct: The canine <u>penchant</u> for hierarchy has its roots in wolf society, which always designated **a canine's** specific role within the pack.

This, Which, and That

The same rule that applies to *it* applies to *this*, *which*, and *that*: each of these pronouns must refer to an antecedent (specific noun, pronoun, or gerund) that appears within the sentence. If the antecedent does not appear, the sentence cannot be correct.

Occasionally, the pronoun *this* will be used without an antecedent.

Incorrect: Australian Jessica Watson became the youngest person ever to sail around the world, completing **this** in March of 2010.

Correct: Australian Jessica Watson became the youngest person ever to sail around the world, completing **her journey** in March of 2010.

Although it is clear in the incorrect version that the word *this* refers to Jessica Watson's journey, the sentence cannot be correct because the noun *journey* does not actually appear in the sentence.

Which is made incorrect in the same way:

Incorrect: Australian Jessica Watson became the youngest person ever to sail around the world, **which** she achieved in March of 2010.

Here again, it is clear from the information provided in the sentence that *which* refers to the feat of sailing around the world. But the noun *sailing* never actually appears – only *to sail*, which is a verb and therefore unable to be an antecedent. In order for the sentence to be correct, we must provide a noun that states exactly what Jessica Watson achieved:

Correct: Australian Jessica Watson became the youngest person ever to sail around the world, **a feat** that she achieved in March of 2010.

Correct: Australian Jessica Watson became the youngest person ever to sail around the world, achieving **that feat** in March of 2010.

Same thing for *that*

Incorrect: Australian Jessica Watson became the youngest person ever to sail around the world, achieving **that** in March of 2010.

Correct: Australian Jessica Watson became the youngest person ever to sail around the world, achieving **that feat** in March of 2010.

In the incorrect version of the sentence, the pronoun *that* does not refer to a specific noun. Only when we supply the noun that it refers to (*feat*) does it become correct.

Pronoun-Antecedent Exercises

In the following sentences, label all pronouns and their antecedents. Some of the sentences may not contain an error. (Answers p. 159, Official Guide question list p. 141)

1. Not until the early twentieth century did the city become capable of maintaining their population and cease to be dependent on rural areas for a constant stream of new inhabitants.

2. Cleota Davis, the mother of jazz legend Miles Davis, was an accomplished pianist in her own right, but she hid that fact from her son until he was an adult.

3. Pain doesn't show up on a body scan and can't be measured in a test, and as a result, many chronic pain sufferers turn to art in an effort to depict that.

4. The nitrogen cycle describes its movement from the air into organic compounds and then back into the atmosphere.

5. If you exercise to prevent diabetes, one may also want to avoid vitamins C and E since these antioxidants have been shown to correlate with it.

6. With the price of art lower, collectors for the most part don't want to part with a prized painting or sculpture unless they are forced to do it.

7. Once common across southwest Asia, the Indian cheetah was driven nearly to extinction during the late twentieth century and now resides in the fragmented pieces of their remaining suitable habitat.

8. Although Alice Sebold does not write her books with any particular age group in mind, it has proven popular with middle and high school students.

9. Some critics of the Internet have argued that it is a danger to people because its vastness, often heralded as a benefit, threatens our intellectual health.

10. The woolly mammoth and the saber-toothed tiger might have survived as late as 10,000 B.C., although it went extinct fairly abruptly right around that time.

11. When the auditorium closes next year for renovations, the theater company will probably hold their productions at another location.

12. While most editors are concerned with how accurate a biography is, others are more interested in how rapidly it can be published.

13. One measure of a society's openness to newcomers is the quality of the space they create for people of unfamiliar cultural and linguistic backgrounds.

14. Though recipes for yeast-free muffins were commonly found in nineteenth-century cookbooks, by the twentieth century most muffin recipes were calling for it.

15. Although the jury spent many hours arguing over the details of the trial, it was ultimately unable to reach a consensus.

16. The Egyptian temple complex at Karnak, situated on the eastern bank of the Nile, was their sacred place of worship.

17. The city's economy has weakened significantly over the past decade, and this has led to an overwhelming loss of manufacturing jobs.

18. In the announcement, the school committee stated that they would substantially overhaul the eleventh grade curriculum at some point during the next year.

19. The world's population could climb to 10.5 billion by 2050, which raises questions about how many people the Earth can support.

20. Paul and Julio had just returned from a long and exhausting hike along the Appalachian Trail when he stumbled and hit his head.

21. In order to become truly great at a sport, players must spend most of his or her free time practicing.

22. Japan's status as an island country means that they must rely heavily on other countries for the supply of natural resources that are indispensable to national existence.

23. The Marquesa islands were among the first South Pacific islands to be settled, and from its shores departed some of the greatest navigators of all time.

24. Google's dominance as an Internet search function has allowed the company to expand their ambitions to include virtually all aspects of the online world.

25. Autobiographies are often structured differently from memoirs, which follow the development of an author's personality rather than the writing of his or her works.

Pronoun Case

Case refers to whether a pronoun is being used as a **subject** or an **object**.

A subject is:

1. the person or thing that is the main focus of the sentence, OR

2. the person or thing performing the action described in the sentence.

In the following sentences, the subject is in bold:

1. **Jonah** read the book.
   (Who read the book? Jonah)

2. **The coat** is more attractive than warm.
   (What is more attractive than it is warm? The coat)

3. Unable to find a place to plug in their computers, **Sarah and Ansel** decided to read instead.
   (Who was unable to find a place to plug in their computers? Sarah and Ansel)

All subjects can be replaced by **subject pronouns**:

I	**We**
You	**You**
She/ He/ It/ One	**They**

If we replace our subjects in the above sentences with pronouns, they become:

1. **Jonah** read the book.
   → **He** read the book.

2. **The coat** is more attractive than warm.
   → **It** is more attractive than warm.

3. Unable to find a place to plug in their computers, **Sarah and Ansel** decided to read instead.
   → Unable to find a place to plug in their computers, **they** decided to read instead.

An **object** is the person or thing that receives an action. In the following sentences, the object is in bold.

1. Jonah read **the book**.
   (What was being read? The book)

2. Akil threw **the basketballs** across the court.
   (What did Akil throw? The basketballs)

3. Serena waved to **Sam and me** from the parking lot.
   (To whom did Serena wave? Sam and me)

All objects can be replaced by **object pronouns**:

Me	**Us**
You	**You**
Her/ Him/ It/ One	**Them**

If we replace the objects in the above sentences with object pronouns, they become:

1. Jonah read **the book**.
    → Jonah read **it.**

2. Akil threw the basketballs across the court.
    → Akil threw **them** across the basketball court.

3. Serena waved to **Sam and me** from the parking lot.
    → Serena waved to **us** from the other side of the parking lot.

Note that proper names (*Serena, Sam, Akil, Sarah*) can be either subjects or objects, but that most pronouns (*I, she, they, them*) can be only one or the other.

Pronoun case errors on the SAT involve only the following subject/object pairs:

I / Me
She, He / Her, Him
We / Us
They / Them

For example, in the sentence *Mary threw the ball to Alisha, Mary* is the subject and *Alisha* is the object. Both are proper names. We can rewrite the sentence several ways to include pronouns:

She threw the ball to Alisha. (*Mary* replaced with object pronoun)

Mary threw the ball to **her**. (*Alisha* replaced with subject pronoun)

She threw the ball to **her**. (*Alisha* replaced with subject pronoun and *Mary* with object pronoun)

What we cannot do, however, is the following:

Her threw the ball to Alisha.

Mary threw the ball to **she**.

Her threw the ball to **she**.

When pronouns are used incorrectly with singular subjects or objects, as in the above sentences, the error is usually pretty easy to spot. Most people clearly would not say, "*My little brother always wants to play with I,*" or "*Him went to the store for some milk.*" But when the subject or object is plural, people tend to get confused. And pronoun case questions will nearly always contain a compound subject or object, usually one with a proper name, that includes the word *and*. For example:

Incorrect: Roosevelt High School's annual prize for citizenship was presented to **Annabel and he** by the vice-principal at the spring awards banquet.

The only thing to remember is that what goes for singular goes for plural. When you see an underlined subject or object pronoun paired with another noun, cross out *and + noun*, and see if the pronoun can stand on its own.

Roosevelt High School's annual prize for citizenship was presented to ~~**Annabel and**~~ **he** by the vice-principal at the spring awards banquet.

Since you would say, *The prize was presented to him* rather than, *The prize was presented to he*, the sentence must be rewritten as follows:

Correct: Roosevelt High School's annual prize for citizenship was presented to **Annabel and him** by the vice-principal at the spring awards banquet.

To reiterate:

Incorrect: After giving a stern lecture on the necessity of checking the validity of our sources, the teacher gave **Jonah and I** back the report we had turned in at the beginning of the week.

In the above sentence, we notice that there is a pronoun paired with a proper name. When we cross out *proper name + and,* we are left with:

Incorrect: After giving a stern lecture on the necessity of checking the validity of our sources, the teacher gave ~~Jonah and~~ **I** back the report we had turned in at the beginning of the week.

Would you say, *The teacher gave I back the report?* Obviously not. So you wouldn't say, *The teacher gave my friend and I back our report* either. But since you would say, *The teacher gave me back the report*, the sentence should read:

Correct: After giving a stern lecture on the necessity of checking the validity of our sources, the teacher gave **Jonah and me** back the report we had turned in at the beginning of the week.

Occasionally, however, an underlined subject or object pronoun will appear without the word *and*.

Incorrect: <u>To</u> **we** students, it seems terribly unfair that school should start at 7:30 a.m.

Correct: <u>To</u> **us** students, it seems terribly unfair that school should start at 7:30 a.m.

When this is the case, there are several ways to determine whether a pronoun is correct.

First, you can use the following rule: **any pronoun that follows a preposition must be an object pronoun.** *We* cannot be correct because it is a subject pronoun, and it follows *to*, which is a preposition.

You can also simply cross out the noun after the pronoun (in this case, *students*). Would you ever say, *To <u>we</u> it seems terribly unfair?* Probably not. So you wouldn't say, *To <u>we</u> students it seems terribly unfair* either.

Important: *Between* is always paired with *me*, NOT with *I*.

Incorrect: Although the start of the movie was delayed, I still missed the first few scenes because the meeting between **my boss and I** ran much later than expected.

Correct: Although the start of the movie was delayed, I still missed the first few scenes because the meeting between **my boss and me** ran much later than expected.

This error is tested frequently on the SAT, and quick recognition of it can save you a lot of time. There are no exceptions to it.

Pronoun Case Exercises

In the following sentences, fix any pronoun case error that appears. Some of the sentences may not contain an error. (Answers p. 160, Official Guide question list p. 143)

1. Although our parents have little difficulty distinguishing between my twin sister and I, our teachers are much more easily fooled by our seemingly identical appearance.

2. For we voters, it is exceedingly difficult to choose between the two candidates because their positions on so many issues are so similar that they are virtually indistinguishable.

3. After listening patiently to our admittedly flimsy excuses, the principal decided to sentence Akiko and I to a week of detention.

4. Along with our project, the professor handed Shalini and I a note requesting that we remain after class in order to discuss our research methods with her.

5. Evidently moved by the strength of their testimony, the jury awarded Tom and him a two million dollar settlement for the injuries they had sustained in the accident.

6. The conversation between my supervisor and me went surprisingly well despite the numerous disputes we had engaged in over the past several weeks.

7. When the gubernatorial candidate arrived at the auditorium to give a speech, we found it nearly impossible to distinguish between she and her assistant, so similar were they in height and appearance.

8. My lab partner and myself were awarded first prize in the science fair for our work on the breakdown of insulin production in people who suffer from diabetes.

9. Walking through Yellowstone National Park, Jordan, Sam, and me were so astonished by our surroundings that we found ourselves at a loss for words.

10. An unfamiliar subject when the class began, Roman history became increasingly fascinating to he and Alexis over the course of the semester.

CUMULATIVE REVIEW #1

The following exercises cover all of the categories discussed thus far. For each sentence, fix the error and label its category. Some sentences may not contain an error. (Answers p. 161)

1. The works of Paulus Barbus has largely been lost, although many editions of his works were both published and esteemed during the Renaissance.

2. Among the writings of linguist Margaret Landon was a dictionary of the Native American Degueño dialect and a comparative study of Central American languages.

3. Many runners, even those who train regularly, do not have a clear sense of their potential since one tends to stick to an established distance.

4. For centuries, Norwegians hang dolls dressed as witches in their kitchens because they believe that such figures have the power to keep pots from burning over.

5. When the fossil of an enormous ancient penguin was unearthed in Peru, archaeologists discovered that their feathers were brown and gray rather than black and white.

6. Although the waiter offered to bring Ramon and I a list of desserts, we had already eaten too much and found the prospect of more food unappetizing.

7. At the meeting point of the Alaskan and the Aleutian mountains rises an immense alpine tundra and sparkling lakes, which give way to thundering waterfalls.

8. Since 1896, the Kentucky Derby – arguably the best-known horse race in America – has took place on a track measuring one-and-a-quarter miles.

9. Sultan Suleyman I, known as Suleyman the Magnificent, has been responsible for the expansion of the Ottoman Empire from Asia Minor to North Africa before his death in 1566.

10. Long Island was the setting for F. Scott Fitzgerald's novel *The Great Gatsby*, but finding traces of them there is as much a job for the imagination as it is for a map and a guidebook.

11. The country's government is so worried about alienating voters that it is proceeding very cautiously in limiting benefits such as unemployment insurance.

12. People who seek out extreme sports such as skydiving and mountain climbing often do so because he or she feels compelled to explore the limits of their endurance.

13. While one is cooking a recipe that involves large quantities of hot chili peppers, you should generally try to avoid touching your eyes.

14. Chicago's Sears Tower was the tallest office building in the world for nearly thirty years, a distinction it has lost only upon the completion of the Taipei 101 Tower in 2004.

41

15. Born in Spain in 1881, Pablo Picasso will become one of the most celebrated and revolutionary painters of the twentieth century because of his invention of the cubist style.

16. The Sherlock Holmes form of mystery novel, which revolve around a baffling crime solved by a master detective and his assistant, contrasts the scientific method with prevailing superstitions.

17. In the early years of the fourteenth century, Pope Clement V moved the papacy to the French city of Avignon and leaving Rome prey to the ambitions of local overlords.

18. Along the side of the winding country road stretch a long line of pine trees and a low, crumbling stone wall covered with both moss and snow.

19. Although the two books recount the same series of events, they do it from different perspectives and are not intended to be read in any particular order.

20. Roberta and her supervisor, Ms. Altschuler, were commended at the company's dinner for her exceptional performance during the previous year.

21. Some of the book's passages wonderfully describe the physical realities of the Middle Ages, while others reflect the dazzling debates that would later lead to the Renaissance.

22. South Africa experienced a series of massive and devastating blackouts in 2008, and consequently they have been rationing electricity ever since that time.

23. Though extremely long, the meeting between my advisor and I was unusually productive because it provided me with many new ways of thinking about a familiar subject.

24. Although prairie dogs were once on the verge of extinction, their numbers have rose to pre-twentieth century levels because of the work of the environmentalists who lobbied for their salvation.

25. In response to be criticized for the poor nutritional value of its food, the restaurant chain has altered its menu to include more healthful options.

3. ADJECTIVES VS. ADVERBS

Adjectives modify nouns or pronouns.

The dog is **wild**.

The wave became **calm**.

It is not **difficult** to accomplish.

Adverbs modify verbs, adjectives, or other adverbs.

He speaks **slowly**.

She runs **very quickly**.

Mr. Samson is a **highly** interesting conversationalist.

Adverbs are usually formed by adding –ly to the adjective.

For adjectives that already end in –y, the adverb is formed by adding –ily.

Adjective	Adverb
Slow	Slowly
Calm	Calmly
Quiet	Quietly
Hasty	Hastily
Noisy	Noisily

Irregularly formed adjectives such as *good* (adj.) → *well* (adv.) are not tested on the SAT.

If there are two consecutive adjectives not separated by a comma, one of the adjectives must often be changed to an adverb.

Incorrect: That book is only **mild** engaging.

Correct: That book is only **mildly** engaging.

On the SAT, adverbs and adjectives are switched only with one another.

If an adjective is underlined, replace it with the adverb; if an adverb is underlined, replace it with the adjective. If the original version is correct, there cannot be an error. Most often, adverbs will be replaced with adjectives, although the reverse does appear occasionally.

Adverb Replaced by Adjective

Incorrect: The patient recovered **quick**, although he had been very ill earlier in the week.

Correct: The patient recovered **quickly**, although he had been very ill earlier in the week.

Adjective Replaced by Adverb

Incorrect: Because the man looked somewhat **oddly**, he received a number of suspicious glances from people who passed him on the street.

Correct: Because the man looked somewhat **odd**, he received a number of suspicious glances from people who passed him on the street.

The incorrect version of the above sentence means that the manner in which the man was performing the act of looking was odd, not that other people perceived his appearance to be odd. While it is grammatically acceptable, its meaning is also highly illogical under normal circumstances.

Adjective vs. Adverb Exercises

For the following exercises, fix any error in adjective or adverb usage. Some of the sentences may not contain an error. (Answers p. 162, Official Guide question list p. 143)

1. In many countries that lack medical workers, citizens with little or no professional preparation have been successfully trained to substitute for doctors and nurses.

2. Explorers who arrived at the central stretch of the Nile River excited reported the discovery of elegant temples and pyramids, ruins of the ancient Kushite civilization.

3. By looking close at DNA markers, scientists may have found traces of the first African hunter-gatherers to migrate to other continents.

4. Although the room appeared tidy at first glance, we saw upon closer inspection that books, pens, and pieces of paper had been scattered haphazard beneath a desk.

5. When examined under a microscope, the beaker of water revealed a hodgepodge of microscopic drifters that looked quite differently from other sea creatures.

6. When Mt. Vesuvius first began to show signs of eruption, many of the people living at the base of the volcano hasty abandoned their villages to seek cover in nearby forests.

7. The archaeologists were lauded for their discovery of the ancient city, once a dense populated urban area that profited from the trade of precious metals.

8. During an era noted for its barbarity, the ancient city of Persepolis, located in modern-day southern Iran, was a relatively cosmopolitan place.

9. Italian nobleman Cesare Borgia was ruthless and vain, but he was also a brilliant Renaissance figure who was exceeding well-educated in the classics.

10. Though few people believe that human beings are entirely rational, a world governed by anti-Enlightenment principles would surely be infinite worse than one governed by Voltaire and Locke.

11. Lake Pergusa, the only natural occurring lake in Sicily, is surrounded by a well-known racing circuit that was created in the 1960's and that has hosted many international sporting events since that time.

12. Even when his theme is the struggle to find a place in a seeming irrational cosmos, Oscar Wilde writes with lively sympathy and hopefulness.

4. PARALLEL STRUCTURE I: LISTS

In any given list or **series** of three or more items, each item should appear in the exact same format: noun, noun, and noun; verb, verb, and verb; or gerund, gerund, and gerund. Any inconsistency is incorrect.

"List" parallelism questions appear primarily in the Error-Identification section, although they do sometimes appear in Fixing Sentences as well.

List with nouns

Incorrect: <u>Changes</u> in wind circulation patterns, <u>runoff</u> from sewage, and **using** chemical fertilizers can lead to the creation of ocean waters low in oxygen and inhospitable to marine life.

Correct: <u>Changes</u> in wind circulation patterns, <u>runoff</u> from sewage, and **use** of chemical fertilizers can lead to the creation of ocean waters low in oxygen and inhospitable to marine life.

List with verbs

Incorrect: When Yukio arrives home from soccer practice, he <u>makes</u> himself a snack, <u>sits</u> down at his desk, and **then he will start** his homework.

Correct: When Yukio arrives home from soccer practice, he <u>makes</u> himself a snack, <u>sits</u> down at his desk, and **starts** his homework.

List with gerunds

Incorrect: Because they have a highly developed sense of vision, most lizards communicate by <u>gesturing</u> with their limbs, <u>changing</u> their colors, or **to display** their athletic abilities.

Correct: Because they have a highly developed sense of vision, most lizards communicate by <u>gesturing</u> with their limbs, <u>changing</u> their colors, or **displaying** their athletic abilities.

Parallel Structure I: List Exercises

In the following sentences, identify and correct any error in parallel structure that appears. Some of the sentences may not contain an error. (Answers p. 162, Official Guide question list p. 144)

1. Lady Jane Grey, known as the nine-day queen, was renowned for her sweetness, her beauty, and being subjected to the whims of her mother.

2. Mediterranean cooking is best known for its reliance on fresh produce, whole grains, and it uses significant amounts of olive oil as well.

3. The biggest beneficiaries of the Grateful Dead archive may prove to be business scholars who are discovering that the Dead were visionaries in the way they created customer value, promoted networking, and implemented strategic business planning.

4. The term "single family house" describes how a house is built and who is intended to live in it, but it does not indicate the house's size, shape, or where it is located.

5. Seeing the Grand Canyon, standing in front of a beautiful piece of art, and to listen to a beautiful symphony are all experiences that may inspire awe.

6. Neighbors of the proposed park argue that an amphitheater would draw more traffic, disrupt their neighborhood, and their only patch of open space would diminish.

7. Evidence suggests that the aging brain retains and even increases its capacity for resilience, growth, and having a sense of well-being.

8. Antiques are typically objects that show some degree of craftsmanship or attention to design, and they are considered desirable because of their beauty, rarity, or being useful.

9. Spiders use a wide range of strategies to capture prey, including trapping it in sticky webs, lassoing it with sticky bolas, and to mimic other insects in order to avoid detection.

10. According to medical authorities at the Mayo Clinic, building muscle can boost metabolism, aiding in weight loss, and increase stamina and focus.

5. PREPOSITIONS AND IDIOMS

Prepositions indicate position, either in terms of **location** or **time**. They are always followed by nouns or pronouns.

> **After** the party
> **On** the table
> **For** me and you

Certain verbs and nouns must be followed by specific prepositions.

Incorrect:	A familiarity **in** Latin is useful for anyone who wishes to pursue serious study of a modern romance language.
Correct:	A familiarity **with** Latin is useful for anyone who wishes to pursue serious study of a modern romance language.

In the above sentence, the phrase *a familiarity* always requires the preposition *with*; any other preposition is incorrect.

A fixed phrase such as *a familiarity with* is known as an **idiom. Idioms are not correct or incorrect for any logical reason; they simply reflect the fact that certain phrases have evolved to be considered standard usage.**

On the SAT, a preposition may also appear where none is necessary.

Incorrect:	The students have been **criticizing about** the administration's decision to begin classes half an hour earlier on most days.
Correct:	The students have been **criticizing** the administration's decision to begin classes half an hour earlier on most days.

In addition, when a sentence contains two verbs that require different prepositions, a separate preposition must follow each verb. Very occasionally, the SAT will omit one of the prepositions.

Incorrect:	After her lecture, the author announced that she would **accept questions** and **respond to** audience members.
Correct:	After her lecture, the author announced that she would **accept questions from** and **respond to** audience members.

Unfortunately, preposition/idiom questions are among the most difficult to study for because there are thousands of possible errors and no real pattern to the prepositions tested. It is therefore not terribly constructive to spend your time memorizing long lists of phrases. In general, though, if a given preposition sounds somewhat odd, it's probably wrong. This is one case that requires you to trust your ear. That said, I am including a list of common idioms, including a number that have appeared on previous tests.

(Pre)occupation with
Consistent/inconsistent with
Sympathize with
Correlate with
Identify with
Familiar/unfamiliar with
In contrast to (BUT: contrast with)
Be native to (BUT: be a native of)
Have a tendency toward
Biased toward
Recommend to
Listen to
Try to (NOT: try and)
Prefer x to y
Devoted to
A threat to/threaten to
Central to
Unique to
Similar to
Parallel to
An alternative to
Enter into
Have insight into
Interested in
Succeed in/at
Adept in/at
Have confidence in
Engage in/with
Take pride in
Insist on
Focus on
Rely on
Reflect on
Dwell on
Draw (up)on
Based on
Suspicious of
Devoid of
A proponent of
A command of
A source of
An offer of
An understanding/knowledge of
Approve/disapprove of
Take advantage of
In awe of
A variety/plethora of

In the hope(s) of
Characteristic/typical of
Convinced of
Consist of
Composed/comprised of
In recognition of
Capable/incapable of
A mastery of
Have an appreciation of/for
Criticize for
Necessary for
Prized for
Endure/last for
Wait for
Watch/look (out) for
Responsible for
Compensate for
Strive for
Have a tolerance for
Famous/Celebrated for
Recognized/known for
Named for/after
Worry about
Complain about
Wonder about
Curious about
Think about
Bring about
Be particular about
Protect from/against
Defend from/against
Apparent from
Predate by
Followed by
Confused/puzzled/perplexed by
Accompanied by
Encouraged by
Outraged by
Surprised/stunned/shocked by
Amazed/awed by
Impressed by
Known as/to be
Far from
Differ(ent) from
Refrain from
Have power/control over
Mull over

Preposition and Idiom Exercises

In the following sentences, identify and correct any preposition error that appears. Some of the sentences may not contain an error. (Answers p. 162, Official Guide question list p. 143)

1. The Wave, a sandstone rock formation located near the Utah-Arizona border, is famous from its colorful outcroppings and rugged, unpaved trails.

2. Frank Lloyd Wright was a proponent for organic architecture, a philosophy that he incorporated into structures such as the Fallingwater residence.

3. Although the author's diaries provide a wealth of information about her daily interests and concerns, they fail to present a comprehensive picture of her life.

4. As an old man, Rousseau acknowledged that it was arrogant of him to promote virtues that he was unable to embody into his own life.

5. The Industrial Revolution, which began toward the end of the eighteenth century, marked the start of the modern era in both Europe and the United States.

6. Beethoven, who strongly sympathized to the ideals of the French Revolution, originally planned to name the *Eroica* symphony after Napoleon.

7. Choreographer Alvin Ailey Jr. is credited in popularizing modern dance and integrating traditional African movements into his works.

8. As a result of its new program, which consists in three world premiers, the ballet troupe has become one of the few eminent companies to promote choreographic innovation.

9. Opposite to his contemporaries, whose work he viewed as conventional and uninspiring, Le Corbusier insisted on using modern industrial techniques to construct buildings.

10. Both bizarre and familiar, fairy tales are intended to be spoken aloud rather than read, and they possess a truly inexhaustible power on children and adults alike.

11. Since reports given by the various witnesses at the crime scene were highly inconsistent with one another, the detective was thoroughly perplexed.

12. Teachers have begun to note with alarm that the amount of time their students spend playing video games and surfing the Internet has severely impacted their ability to focus at a single task for an extended period of time.

13. During the early decades of the Heian Empire, a person who lacked a thorough knowledge in Chinese could never be considered fully educated.

14. Created in Jamaica during the late 1960's, reggae music emerged out of a number of sources that ranged from traditional African songs and chants to contemporary jazz and blues.

15. In "Howl" as well as in his other poetry, Allen Ginsberg drew inspiration from the epic, free verse style associated to the nineteenth century poet Walt Whitman.

6. FAULTY COMPARISONS

Faulty Comparison questions appear primarily in the Error-Identification section, typically in the last three questions and often in question #27. They do, however, also appear in Fixing Sentences, usually in the last three questions as well. The general rule for forming comparisons is as follows:

Compare things to things and people to people.

Faulty comparisons can often be anticipated by the presence of a comparison such as *more than*, *less than*, or *(un)like*.

Singular faulty comparison

Incorrect: In twentieth century America, Norman Rockwell's art was better known than Russian painter Wassily Kandinsky.

In the above sentence, art (a thing) is being compared to Wassily Kandinsky (a person). In order to make the sentence correct, art must be compared to art. Most people will instinctively correct the sentence as follows:

In twentieth century America, Norman Rockwell's **art** was better known than Russian painter **Wassily Kandinsky's art.**

The SAT, however, will ask you to fix such errors with the phrase *that of* when they appear in Fixing Sentences.

Correct: In twentieth century America, Norman Rockwell's **art** was better known than **that of** Russian painter Wassily Kandinsky.

BUT NOT: In twentieth century America, Norman Rockwell's **art** was better known than **that of** Russian painter **Wassily Kandinsky's.** (= the art of Wassily Kandinsky's *art*)

Plural faulty comparison

A plural faulty comparison should be corrected with the phrase *those of*.

Incorrect: In Victorian England, Charles Dickens' **novels** were more widely read than **Victor Hugo**.

Correct: In Victorian England, Charles Dickens' **novels** were more widely read than **those of** Victor Hugo.

BUT NOT: In Victorian England, Charles Dickens' **novels** were more widely read than **those of** **Victor Hugo's.** (= the novels of Victor Hugo's *novels*)

Important: the inclusion of an author or artist's name in a sentence often indicates a faulty comparison.

Exception to the Person vs. Thing Rule

Occasionally, the SAT will throw in a faulty comparison that does not involve comparing things and people but rather two things. In such cases, you must make sure that the two things being compared are truly equivalent.

Incorrect: Unlike a train, the length of a tram is usually limited to one or two cars, which may run either on train tracks or directly on the street.

What is being compared here?

1) A train

2) The length of a tram

Even though both *train* and *length* are nouns, they are not equivalent. We must either compare a train to a train or a length to a length.

Correct: Unlike **the length of** a train, the length of a tram is usually limited to one or two cars, which may run either on train tracks or directly on the street.

Correct: Unlike **that of** a train, the length of a tram is usually limited to one or two cars, which may run either on train tracks or directly on the street.

Faulty Comparison Exercises

In the following sentences, identify and correct any faulty comparison that appears. Some of the sentences may not contain an error. (Answers p. 163, Official Guide question list p. 145)

1. The writings of John Locke, unlike Thomas Hobbes, emphasize the idea that people are by nature both reasonable and tolerant.

2. Company officials announced that there would be no major changes made to the eligibility requirements for its benefits package, an offering that makes its plan more generous than other major retailers.

3. As part of its application, the university asks students to compose a short essay in which they compare their educational interests and goals to that of other students.

4. The humor in Lynne Shelton's film *Touchy Feely* is softer and more ambiguous than her earlier films, and its characters' transformations are sharper and more difficult to comprehend.

5. Unlike dyslexia, people with dysgraphia often suffer from fine motor-skills problems that leave them unable to write clearly.

6. Today's neuroscientists, unlike thirty years ago, have access to sophisticated instrumentation that has only been developed over the past decade.

7. Norwegian doctors prescribe fewer antibiotics than any other country, so people do not have a chance to develop resistance to many kinds of drug-resistant infections.

8. Archaeologists have long been far more puzzled by members of the Saqqaq culture, the oldest known inhabitants of Greenland, than by those of other prehistoric North American cultures.

9. The reproduction of ciliates, unlike other organisms, occurs when a specimen splits in half and grows a completely new individual from each piece.

10. The hands and feet of Ardi, the recently discovered human ancestor who lived 4.4 million years ago, are much like other primitive extinct apes.

11. At the age of twenty-four, playwright Thornton Wilder was balding and bespectacled, and his clothes were like a much older man.

12. In ancient Greece, women were not allowed to vote or hold property, their status differing from slaves only in name.

7. WORD PAIRS

On the SAT, the following pairs of words (or **correlative conjunctions**) must appear together; any deviation is considered incorrect. While the following list is fairly extensive, *(n)either…(n)or*, *not only…but also*, and *as…as* are the most commonly tested pairs, and you should therefore focus on learning them first.

A. Either…or

Either the company's president **or** her assistant will be present at the press conference scheduled for later this afternoon.

B. Neither…nor

According to the politician, **neither** the recent crisis **nor** any other period of economic turmoil had been caused by environmental protection policies.

C. Not only…but also

Apples **not only** taste very good, **but** they **also** contain numerous essential vitamins and minerals.

D. Both
Between ⎤ and
At once ⎦

The news station, while successful, trails its competitor in **both** the morning **and** the evening news broadcast.

When purchasing a computer, many people find it difficult to decide **between** buying a Macintosh **and** buying a different brand.

The politician is **at once** controversial because of his refusal to compromise **and** beloved because of his personal charisma.

E. As
Not so much ⎦ as

Although she began training later than many other gymnasts, Jessica is just **as** good an athlete **as** most of her competitors.

Although her plays have garnered praise from many critics, Toni Morrison is known **not so much** for her theatrical works **as** she is for her novels.

54

F.
So
Such   } that

The first lesula monkey seen by researchers bore a strong resemblance to the owl-faced monkey, but **so** unusual was the lesula monkey's coloring **that** they suspected it was a new species.

The first lesula monkey seen by researchers bore a strong resemblance to the owl-faced monkey, but the lesula monkey had **such** unusual coloring **that** they suspected it was a new species.

G.
More
Less   } than
No sooner

Although Jane Austen's novels are **more** widely read **than** those of her contemporaries, Austen was hardly the only female author in nineteenth-century England.

No sooner had the senator announced her intention not to run for re-election **than** the media began to speculate about the next stage of her political career.

H. From…to

The shift **from** monarchy **to** totalitarianism occurred in Russia over a remarkably short period of time in the early twentieth century.

I. Just as…so

Just as Thomas Edison is known for inventing the electric light bulb, **so** is Albert Einstein known for developing a theory of general relativity.

J.
Only when
Only after   } did*
Not until

Only when/after negotiations began **did** workers and managers realize the extent of their disagreements.

Not until negotiations began **did** workers and managers realize the extent of their disagreements.

K.
It was only when
It was only after   } that
It was not until

It was only when/after negotiations began **that** workers and managers realized the extent of their disagreements.

It was not until negotiations began **that** workers and managers realized the extent of their disagreements.

*Although *did* is almost always paired with the words listed here, a form of *to be* or *to have* can also be used with a passive construction (e.g. *Not until the police arrived at the museum <u>was</u> it discovered that the thief had escaped with several smaller paintings in addition to the large masterpiece*, OR: *Not until now <u>have</u> the effects of the chemical truly been understood*).

Word Pair Exercises

In the following sentences, identify and correct any word pair error that appears. Some of the sentences may not contain an error. (Answers p. 163, Official Guide question list p. 145)

1. Known for his designs inspired by natural principles, architect Michael Pawlyn was initially torn between architecture or biology but eventually chose the former.

2. After weeks of unproductive negotiations, workers have finally agreed to discuss the overtime dispute with both outside mediators plus company officials.

3. Once stereotyped as savants because of their depictions in movies such as *Rain Man*, people on the autistic spectrum are typically neither superhuman memory machines or incapable of performing everyday tasks.

4. Obedience to authority is not only a way for rulers to keep order in totalitarian states, and it is the foundation on which such states exist.

5. In the Middle Ages, the term "arts" referred to a wide range of fields including geometry, grammar, and astronomy; only in the nineteenth century did it come to denote painting, drawing, and sculpting.

6. Audiences find the play at once amusing because of the comedic skills of its leading actors, but it is also tedious because of its excessive length.

7. It is almost as difficult to find consistent information about the Fort Pillow incident during the American Civil War than it is to determine the significance of its outcome.

8. So great was the surplus of food created by the ancient Mesopotamians that it led to the establishment of the first complex civilization in human history.

9. Because the Articles of Confederation did not provide for the creation of either executive agencies and judiciary institutions, they were rejected in favor of the Constitution.

10. Just as moral intelligence, an innate sense of right and wrong, allowed human societies to flourish, so did a strong sense of hierarchy allow canine societies to thrive.

11. One of the main effects of industrialization was the shift from a society in which women worked at home with one in which women worked in factories and brought home wages to their families.

12. Over the past decade, Internet usage has become so pervasive and many psychologists are beginning to study its effects on the lives of children and adolescents.

13. It was not until the late seventeenth century when some English writers began to challenge the traditional view of commerce, which held that money-making was a source of moral corruption to be avoided at all cost.

14. Just as the machine age transformed an economy of farm laborers and artisans into one of assembly lines, so the technology revolution is replacing factory workers with robots and clerks with computers.

15. Although Voltaire wrote a number of tragedies and believed he would be remembered as a dramatist, he is known today not so much for his theatrical works than he is for his satires.

CUMULATIVE REVIEW #2

The following exercises cover all of the categories discussed thus far. For each sentence, fix the error and label its category. Some sentences may not contain an error. (Answers p. 164)

1. Three million years ago, the creation of the Panama Isthmus wreaked ecological havoc by triggering extinctions, diverting ocean currents, and it also transformed the climate.

2. The professor's appearance was very striking to everyone in the room, for not only was he extremely thin, but his height also surpassed a normal man.

3. Although many children want to read digitized books and would read for fun more frequent if they could obtain them, most claim that do not want to give up traditional print books completely.

4. Before Staughton Lynd vanished from intellectual society, he was one of the most recognizable and controversial thinkers that the United States had ever produced.

5. Although clarinetist Artie Shaw spent far more of his long life writing prose than making music, a careful look at his compositions reveal that he was a musician of genius.

6. Among the earliest complex civilizations in Mexico were the Olmec culture, which flourished on the gulf coast beginning in around 1500 BCE.

7. Although the movie has alternately been described as a social satire, a comedy of manners, and being a Greek tragedy, it contains elements of all three.

8. In the early nineteenth century, a number of adventurous artists and writers flocked to Lake Geneva to savor about its inspiring mountain scenery and serene atmosphere.

9. Parrots are not only capable of mimicking human speech but in some cases also demonstrate the ability to form associations between words with their meanings.

10. *The Europeans*, a short novel by Henry James, contrasts the behavior and attitudes of two visitors from Italy with their cousins from New England.

11. Thomas Jefferson believed that prisoners of war should be treated humane and, during the American Revolution, requested that British and Hessian generals be held in mansions rather than behind bars.

12. Ten years after Native American chief Squanto had been kidnapped and brought to Spain, he returned home and befriended some of the first English colonists.

13. A rebellion from the rigid academic art that predominated during the nineteenth century, the Art Nouveau movement was inspired by natural forms and structures.

14. Although the best-selling author had grew comfortable with her role as a public figure, when given the choice, she preferred to be alone.

15. While reactions to the exhibition were mixed, neither the artist's exceptional showmanship nor his astonishing technique were questioned by the spectators.

16. Unlike Nathaniel Hawthorne and F. Scott Fitzgerald, Jonathan Franzen's novels have not yet received unanimous acceptance as classic works of literature.

17. Supporters of bilingual education often imply that students miss a great deal by not to be taught in the language spoken by their parents and siblings at home.

18. A small frontier town in the 1830's, Chicago had grown to more than two million residents by 1909, and some demographers predicted that it will soon be the largest city on earth.

19. John Breckinridge, who came closest in defeating Abraham Lincoln in the 1860 election, held strong personal convictions that made it difficult for him to navigate a moderate course in an era of extremes.

20. According to many urban planners, the most efficient way of building prosperous cities is to make it not only attractive but also healthy.

21. The origin of the senators' proposal dates to the mid-twentieth century, making it one of the most eager anticipated pieces of legislation this year.

22. Societies located at river deltas tend to foster innovation because of their flexibility to deal with potentially shifting landscapes.

23. In general, the design and management of highways and parking lots are handed over to traffic engineers, whose decisions heavily influence people's behavior within those spaces.

24. The City Beautiful movement, which swept America during the late nineteenth century, was embodied in the stately lines, formal balance, and grand scale of the buildings constructed during that period.

25. When the Cooper Union for the Advancement of Science and Art opened its doors in 1859, it represented for Peter Cooper the realization of an idea that had occupied his imagination for nearly thirty years.

8. NOUN AGREEMENT

Nouns must agree in number when they are connected by a **linking verb** such as *to be* or *to become*: singular subjects must go with singular nouns, and plural subjects must go with plural nouns.

Singular noun agreement

Incorrect: After visiting the physics laboratory with their class, <u>Michael and Lakeisha</u> were inspired to become **a scientific researcher** when they grew up.

Correct: After visiting the physics laboratory with their class, <u>Michael and Lakeisha</u> were inspired to become **scientific researchers** when they grew up.

Plural noun agreement

Usually, the SAT will pair a plural subject with a singular noun, as in the above sentence. Occasionally, however, it will pair a singular subject with a plural noun.

Incorrect: <u>Mozart</u>, along with Haydn and Beethoven, were **members** of the First Viennese School of classical music.

Correct: <u>Mozart</u>, along with Haydn and Beethoven, was **a member** of the First Viennese School of classical music.

You can identify and correct such sentences by treating them as simple subject-verb agreement questions. Since the sentences contains a non-essential clause, simply cross out the clause and the error will reveal itself:

Mozart…were members of the First Viennese School of classical music.

Since Mozart is one person, he must have been *a member* rather than *members* of the First Viennese School.

Important: Sentences testing noun agreement will often include phrase *as a + profession* (e.g. writer, scientist, photographer). Any time a profession is mentioned, check the noun agreement first.

Noun agreement and faulty comparison errors are the only two common errors that involve underlined nouns. In virtually all other cases, underlined nouns can be automatically eliminated as error options.

Noun Agreement Exercises

In the following sentences, identify and correct any noun agreement error that appears. Some of the sentences may not contain an error. (Answers p. 165, Official Guide question list p. 145)

1. Both Wilfrid Daniels and Leonard Chuene, now powerful figures in South African sports, grew up as a promising athlete who could never compete internationally because of apartheid.

2. Because they evolved in the warm climate of Africa before spreading into Europe, modern humans had a body adapted to tracking prey over great distances.

3. Many of the great classical composers, including Mozart, Bach, and Mendelssohn, were born into musical families and began studying an instrument seriously when they were a child.

4. Thomas Abercrombie, along with his older brother, became a photographer after building a camera out of mirrors, discarded lenses, and scraps of plastic.

5. Known for creating a unique sound and style through the use of non-traditional instruments such as the French horn, Miles Davis joined Louis Armstrong and Ella Fitzgerald as the greatest jazz musicians of the twentieth century.

6. Inscribed ostrich eggs and pieces of shell jewelry are an example of early human attempts to record thoughts symbolically rather than literally.

7. Joseph Charles Jones and George Bundy Smith, who fought for African-Americans as a civil rights activist during the early 1960's, were separated for nearly forty years after being arrested in Alabama in 1961.

8. The Opium Wars, which introduced the power of western armies and technologies to China, marked the end of Shanghai and Ningpo as an independent port city.

9. Although neither came from a literary family, novelists Amy Tan and Maxine Hong Kingston became an avid reader while growing up near San Francisco.

10. The military and the orchestra are examples of distinct entities that must interact with their own subsystems or units in order to survive.

9. COMPARATIVES VS. SUPERLATIVES

Comparative

Comparative = -ER form of adjective or *MORE + ADJECTIVE*

    Examples: smaller, larger, faster, brighter, more interesting, more exciting

Comparatives are used only when comparing **two** things:

    Incorrect: Between the rhino and the hippo, the rhino is the **heavier** creature, while the hippo is the **most** ferocious.

    Correct: Between the rhino and the hippo, the rhino is the **heavier** creature, while the hippo is the **more** ferocious.

Superlative

Superlative = -EST form of adjective or *MOST + ADJECTIVE*

    Examples: smallest, largest, fastest, brightest, most interesting, most exciting

Superlative are used only when comparing **three or more** things:

    Incorrect: The executive interviewed <u>five</u> candidates for the position and ultimately decided that Sergei was the **more** qualified.

    Correct: The executive interviewed <u>five</u> candidates for the position and ultimately decided that Sergei was the **most** qualified.

Important: Whenever you see a comparative underlined, replace it with the superlative and vice-versa. Comparatives and superlatives are switched only with one another.

Comparative vs. Superlative Exercises

In the following sentences, identify and correct any error in the use of comparatives or superlatives. Some of the sentences may not contain an error. (Answers p. 166, Official Guide question list p. 146)

1. Between the black leopard and the snow leopard, the black leopard possesses the more effective camouflage while the snow leopard has the most striking tail.

2. Of the two top-ranked players on the university's tennis team, Ken is seen as the more likely candidate for a national championship.

3. Asked to choose between Gary Kasparov and Bobby Fischer, most chess experts would declare Fischer to be the better player.

4. While triathlons, competitions that consist of swimming, biking, and running, are drawing increasing numbers of participants, athletic events devoted to a single sport remain most popular.

5. Although many viewers find his work on color and geometric shapes to be excessively abstract and inaccessible, Paul Klee is nonetheless regarded as one of the most innovative artists of the early twentieth century.

6. Confronted with two equally qualified finalists, the awards committee is struggling to determine which one is most deserving of the top prize.

7. When the influenza virus, one of the most commonly diagnosed diseases in the United States, was formally recognized in 1933, many doctors believed that a cure would be found shortly.

8. Though London has a longstanding reputation as a city whose weather is defined by rain and fog, in reality Paris receives the highest amount of rainfall each year.

9. Both poodles and pugs are known for making excellent pets, but between the two breeds, pugs have the sweetest disposition while poodles are smarter.

10. Although mental puzzles such as Sudoku can help people keep their minds nimble as they age, physical exercise such as biking or running is most effective.

10. RELATIVE PRONOUNS:
Who, Which, When, Where & That

Who(m) vs. Which

Use *who* or *whom*, not *which*, when referring to people.*

Incorrect:	King Henry VIII was a British <u>monarch</u> **which** ruled England during the Tudor period and was known for his many wives.
Correct:	King Henry VIII was a British <u>monarch</u> **who** ruled England during the Tudor period and was known for his many wives.

Very Important: *who vs. whom* is **not** tested on the SAT. If *whom* is underlined, ignore it. That said, *which* will very occasionally be used incorrectly to replace *whom* rather than *who*. You will, however, only be responsible for recognizing that *which* is being incorrectly used to refer to a person.

Incorrect:	The members of the youth orchestra, **many of which** have been studying music since a very young age, are frequently praised for the exceptional quality of their playing.
Correct:	The members of the youth orchestra, **many of whom** have been studying music since a very young age, are frequently praised for the exceptional quality of their playing.

Whom is used to refer to a person or people, and in the above sentence, it is the object of the preposition *of*.

Which vs. That

Which = Comma

That = No comma

Which is always preceded by a comma and is used to set off a non-essential clause.

Incorrect:	The movie, **that** opened last Friday, has earned rave reviews from critics and fans alike.
Correct:	The movie, **which** opened last Friday, has earned rave reviews from critics and fans alike.

That is never preceded by a comma and is used to set off an essential clause.

Incorrect:	The movie **which** opened last Friday has earned rave reviews from critics and fans alike.
Correct:	The movie **that** opened last Friday has earned rave reviews from critics and fans alike.

*Although *that* can also be used to refer to people, the SAT generally prefers *who*. *Who vs. that* is not tested, however.

Where

Where is for places (physical locations) only. To refer to books, use *in which*.

Incorrect: The novel *Life of Pi*, written by Yann Martel, is a story **where** the protagonist survives on a raft in the ocean for nearly a year, accompanied only by a tiger.

Correct: The novel *Life of Pi*, written by Yann Martel, is a story **in which** the protagonist survives on a raft in the ocean for nearly a year, accompanied only by a tiger.

When a place is being referred to, however, *where* and *in which* are equally acceptable. *In which* is simply a bit more formal.

Correct: Although Einstein predicted the presence of black holes, regions of space **where** gravity is so intense that not even light can escape, he had difficulty believing that they could actually exist.

Correct: Although Einstein predicted the presence of black holes, regions of space **in which** gravity is so intense that not even light can escape, he had difficulty believing that they could actually exist.

When

When is for times/time periods.

Incorrect: The Middle Ages was a period **where** many farmers were bound to the lands they worked.

Correct: The Middle Ages was a period **when** many farmers were bound to the lands they worked.

Preposition + which is also acceptable.

Correct: The Middle Ages was a period **in/during which** many farmers were bound to the lands they worked.

Important: although the word *which* will often be wrong when it appears by itself, the construction *preposition + which* will virtually always be correct when it is underlined in the Error-Identification section.

Relative Pronoun Exercises

In the following sentences, identify and correct any relative pronoun error that appears. Some of the sentences may not contain an error. (Answers p. 166, Official Guide question list p. 146)

1. For delicate patients which cannot handle the rigors of modern medicine, some doctors are now rejecting the assembly line of modern medical care for older, gentler options.

2. In its later years, the Bauhaus architectural movement became a kind of religion in which heretics had to be excommunicated by those who held the true light.

3. When readers which get their news from electronic rather than printed sources send articles to their friends, they tend to choose ones that contain intellectually challenging topics.

4. In 1623, Galileo published a work where he championed the controversial theory of heliocentrism, thus provoking one of the greatest scientific controversies of his day.

5. In classical Athenian democracy, citizens which failed to pay their debts were barred from attending assembly meetings and appearing in court in virtually any capacity.

6. Carol Bove, an artist who is known for her drawings and installations concerning the social and political movements of the 1960's, often found inspiration for her work in vintage books and magazines.

7. Researchers have claimed that subjects which stood on a rapidly vibrating platform during an experiment were able to slightly improve their athletic performance for a short time afterward.

8. In his utopian novel *Walden Two*, B.F. Skinner invents a world in which emotions such as envy have become obsolete because people are conditioned as children to reject them.

9. One of the least popular of all the Romance languages, Romansch is traditionally spoken by people which inhabit the southern regions of Switzerland.

10. The wave of fascination greeting the film's release is a phenomenon that seems worthy of attention, regardless of the movie's artistic merit.

11. DOUBLE NEGATIVES AND DOUBLE POSITIVES

Double Negative

Always use *any* with the words *scarcely* and *hardly*. On the SAT, *any* will usually be incorrectly replaced with *no*.

Incorrect: When I looked in the refrigerator, I realized that there was **scarcely/hardly no** milk left.

Correct: When I looked in the refrigerator, I realized that there was **scarcely/hardly any** milk left.

Double Positive

Never use *more* or *most* in addition to the comparative or superlative form of an adjective.

Comparative

Incorrect: When traveling over large distances, most people choose to go by airplane rather than by train because the airplane is the **more faster** option.

Correct: When traveling over large distances, most people choose to go by airplane rather than by train because the airplane is the **faster** option.

Superlative

Incorrect: Imitation, long considered the **most sincerest** form of flattery, may carry evolutionary benefits for both model and mimic alike.

Correct: Imitation, long considered the **sincerest** form of flattery, may carry evolutionary benefits for both model and mimic alike.

Double Negative and Double Positive Exercises

In the following sentences, identify and correct any double negative or double positive error that appears. Some of the sentences may not contain an error. (Answers p. 166, Official Guide question list p. 146)

1. When selecting a host city from among dozens of contenders, Olympic officials must take into consideration which one is most likeliest to benefit from the legacy of the games.

2. Although the plays of Lillian Hellman and Bertolt Brecht were met with great popularity during the 1920's, they are scarcely never performed anymore in the United States.

3. Since the advent of commercial flight and high-speed rail in the twentieth century, hardly no significant technological change has affected the traveling public.

4. An evolutionary adaptation that might have promised survival during prehistoric times is more likelier nowadays to produce diseases in modern humans.

5. Though the Panama Canal is hardly new, having opened nearly a hundred years ago, the idea of a waterway connecting the Atlantic and Pacific Oceans is significantly older than the canal itself.

6. The Indian sub-continent was home to some of the most earliest civilizations, ranging from urban society of the Indus Valley to the classical age of the Gupta Dynasty.

7. During the early days of cable television, many viewers were only able to access four channels, with reception being weakest in rural areas and most clearest in large cities.

8. The Industrial Revolution, which began in the late 1700's and lasted more than fifty years, was the period when machine power became more stronger than hand power.

9. Although many people have attempted to solve the mystery of Stonehenge, its purpose is hardly any clearer than it was centuries ago.

10. To thoroughly understand historical figures, we must study them not only in the bright light of the present but also in the more cloudier light of the circumstances they encountered in their own lifetimes.

12. CONJUNCTIONS

Conjunction questions test your ability to recognize logical connections between ideas.

There are three main types of conjunctions:

Continuers

Continuers are words such as *and*, *in addition*, *furthermore*, and *moreover*, which indicate that a sentence is continuing in the direction it began. The main continuer that appears in the Error-Identification section is *and*.

> Continuer: The sun streamed through the window into the living room, **and** its brightness was so great that it lit up the hall as well.

Contradictors

Contradictors are words such as *but*, *yet*, *although*, and *however* that indicate a sentence is shifting directions or introducing contradictory information.

> Contradictor: To remove about a quarter of a long, complicated book was close to an impossible task, **but** over the course of several months, the author accomplished it.

> Contradictor: To remove about a quarter of a long, complicated book was close to an impossible task; **however,** over the course of several months, the author accomplished it.

Cause and Effect

Common examples are *so*, *for*, *therefore*, *because*, and *since*. They indicate that an action or occurrence is causing a particular result, or that a particular result is occurring because of an action or occurrence.

> Cause/Effect: The first astronauts were required to undergo mental evaluation before their flight **because** the psychological danger inherent in space travel was judged to be as important as the physiological one.

There are two main kinds of conjunction errors:

1) Incorrect Conjunction Type

2) Double Conjunction

Incorrect Conjunction Type

In this error, a contradictor is most often replaced with a continuer:

Incorrect: Many runners attempt to complete a marathon, **and** many fail to do so because they lack the necessary stamina.

Correct: Many runners attempt to complete a marathon, **but** many fail to do so because they lack the necessary stamina.

An underlined conjunction in the Error-Identification section can signal a conjunction error. To figure out the relationship between the clauses and thus the correct conjunction, cross out the existing conjunction in order to avoid being prejudiced by it, then ask yourself whether the clauses express the same idea or opposing ideas.

Clause 1:   Many runners attempt to complete a marathon.

Clause 2:   Many fail to do so because they lack the necessary stamina.

Clearly, the second clause presents an opposing idea (*they fail to do so*), and therefore a transition that indicates opposition (*but*) is required.

Watch out for "when"

Sometimes, however, the relationship between the two clauses will be made less obvious, a trick that is often accomplished by replacing a clear-cut continuer or contradictor such as *and* or *but* with *when*. I call *when* a "dummy" conjunction because it sounds just odd enough that most test-takers can sense that something isn't quite right but not so obviously wrong that they can necessarily put their finger on the problem. For example:

Incorrect: Santiago's failure to complete the marathon surprised no one, least of all his training partners, **when** he had not spent enough time building the necessary stamina.

At first reading, the sentence may sound somewhat strange, but it is difficult to identify precisely why. At this point, the goal is to simplify the sentence into a more manageable form. If we consider the structure of the sentence, we notice that there are two commas in the interior of the sentence, indicating a non-essential clause. If we remove the non-essential clause, we are left with the following:

Santiago's failure to complete the marathon surprised no one, **when** he had not spent enough time building the necessary stamina.

Clearly, the fact that Santiago didn't complete the marathon is a <u>result</u> of his failure to build the necessary stamina, so a transition such as *for* or *because* is required.

Correct: Santiago's failure to complete the marathon surprised no one, least of all his training partners, **for** he had not spent enough time building the necessary stamina.

Correct: Santiago's failure to complete the marathon surprised no one, least of all his training partners **because** he had not spent enough time building the necessary stamina.

Double Conjunction

Only one conjunction is typically necessary to connect two clauses. The SAT will occasionally make a sentence incorrect by adding an extra conjunction where it is not needed.

Incorrect: **Although** Santiago had trained hard for the marathon, **but** he was unable to finish the entire course.

Correct: **Although** Santiago had trained hard for the marathon, he was unable to finish the entire course.

Correct: Santiago had trained hard for the marathon, **but** he was unable to finish the entire course.

The SAT will only give you the option of removing one of the conjunctions; you will never have to choose between them.

Conjunction Exercises

In the following sentences, identify and correct any conjunction error that appears. Some of the sentences may not contain an error. (Answers p. 167, Official Guide question list p. 146)

1. In the past, coffees were blended and branded to suit a homogenous popular taste, and that has recently changed in response to a growing awareness of regional differences.

2. Since Frederic Chopin's charming and sociable personality drew loyal groups of friends and admirers, including George Sand, but his private life was often painful and difficult.

3. The Taj Mahal is regarded as one of the eight wonders of the world, although some historians have noted that its architectural beauty has never been surpassed.

4. Music serves no obvious evolutionary purpose when it has been, and remains, part of every known civilization on earth.

5. There is no escaping the fact that most of the world's big cats are in serious trouble because of poaching, and tigers are no exception to this situation.

6. Although saving an endangered species requires preservationists to study it in detail, but unfortunately scientific information about some animals is scarce.

7. Pyramids are most commonly associated with ancient Egypt, so it comes as a surprise to many people that Nubian civilization, located in modern-day Sudan, produced far more pyramids than Egyptian civilization ever did.

8. Modern chemistry keeps insects from ravaging crops, lifts stains from carpets, and saves lives, and the constant exposure to chemicals is taking a toll on many people's health.

9. If people were truly at home under the light of the moon and stars, they would live happily in darkness, and their eyes are adapted to living in the sun's light.

10. No one truly knows where the pirate known as Blackbeard called home, but author Daniel Defoe, a self-appointed piracy expert, claimed that he came from the English city of Bristol.

11. Roman women could only exercise political power through men, the only people considered true citizens, when they were not allowed to participate directly in politics.

CUMULATIVE REVIEW #3

The following exercises cover all of the categories discussed thus far. For each sentence, fix the error and label its category. Some sentences may not contain an error. (Answers p. 167)

1. In their stories, originally published in the eighteenth century, the Brothers Grimm have embraced a number of themes that have never vanished from life, despite modern advances in science and technology.

2. The flexible scales around the side of the shortfin mako shark allow it to swiftly change direction while maintaining a high speed.

3. Entomologists have identified the jewel beetle and the fire-chaser beetle as an insect that can thrive in trees scorched by wildfires or destroyed by other natural disasters.

4. Objectivity, one of the central values of science, is based on the idea that scientists must aspire to eliminate all his or her personal biases in attempting to uncover truths about the natural world.

5. A recently undertaken survey of drivers and cyclists has revealed that, compared to drivers, cyclists are most likely to use hand signals.

6. Lan Samantha Chang is a critically acclaimed novelist which counts among her influences authors as varied as Charlotte Brontë and Edgar Allan Poe.

7. In response to their critics, advocates of genetically modified foods typically insist that such crops grow faster, require fewer pesticides, and they are reducing stress on natural resources.

8. Much like human beings, wolves are capable of exerting a profound influence on the environments that it inhabits.

9. Giant galaxies like the Milky Way and the nearby Andromeda galaxy, which is even more larger, possess the power to create and retain a wide variety of elements.

10. Many scientists are baffled from the appearance of Yersinia pestis, a fungus that has been destroying bat populations throughout the United States in recent years.

11. Migrating animals maintain a fervid attentiveness that allows them to be neither distracted by temptations or deterred by challenges that would turn other animals aside.

12. For all the fear and loathing Aztec rulers instilled in the inhabitants of the regions that they conquered, their power was ultimately short-lived.

13. Dumping pollution in oceans not only adds to the unsightliness of the formerly pristine waters, and it destroys the marine life that inhabits them.

14. Between 1903 and 1913, the British suffragettes, a group devoted to helping women win the right to vote, resorted to increasingly extreme measures to make their voices heard.

72

15. When it was first built, the Spanish Armada was said to be invincible, a designation that quickly became ironic since it was destroyed by the British in hardly no time.

16. Pottery is made by forming clay into various shapes and heating it to high temperatures in a kiln, inducing permanent changes that include increasing the clay's strength and setting its form.

17. Construction on the Great Wall of China began many thousands of years ago and initially involving the creation of hundreds of miles of fortresses to defend against foreign invaders.

18. The earliest surviving guitars date from the sixteenth century, and images of guitar-like instruments were depicted in Egyptian paintings and murals as early as 1900 B.C.

19. The women in the nearly century-old photograph seemed strangely familiar to Shayla and I, but try as we might, we could not recall where we had seen them before.

20. A new generation of powerful digital tools and databases are transforming the study of literature, philosophy, and other humanistic fields.

21. Under the feudal system, which prevailed in Europe during the Middle Ages, the status of an individual and his or her interactions with members of different social classes were rigidly specified.

22. Well into the twentieth century, to defend the notion of full social and political equality for all members of society was being considered a fool.

23. Although George Washington and General Lafayette were great friends, they came from wide disparate backgrounds and had little in common.

24. The great ancient city of Tenochtitlan was in many ways a repository of customs, images, and practices borrowed from previous civilizations.

25. Although birds are not generally known for their intelligence, recent findings have established that parrots often possess skills similar to human toddlers.

13. REDUNDANCY

Redundancy errors occur rarely, but they can appear in both the Error-Identification and Fixing Sentences sections.

Incorrect: The upper basin of Utah's Lake Powell provides a minimum **annual** flow of eight million tons of water **per year** to states across the Southwest.

Correct: The upper basin of Utah's Lake Powell provides a minimum **annual** flow of eight million tons of water to states across the Southwest.

Correct: The upper basin of Utah's Lake Powell provides a minimum flow of eight million tons of water **per year** to states across the Southwest.

Since annual and per year mean exactly the same thing, it is unnecessary to include both in the sentence. Either one by itself is correct.

Redundancy Exercises

In the following sentence, identify and underline redundant words or phrases that may appear. Some sentences may not contain an error. (Answers p. 168, Official Guide question p. 150)

1. *Glengarry Glen Ross* earned David Mamet a Pulitzer Prize in 1984, eight years after a trio of off-Broadway plays initially garnered him major acclaim for the first time.

2. Although the students in the auditorium were silent throughout the entire lecture, the professor spoke so softly that his voice was nearly inaudible and could hardly be heard.

3. Scuba divers usually move around underwater by using fins attached to their feet, but external propulsion can be provided from an outside source by a specialized propulsion vehicle or a sled pulled from the surface.

4. Accused of purposefully neglecting to follow crucial steps in the laboratory's safety protocol, the researcher insisted that the oversight was inadvertent and had occurred entirely by accident.

5. Faced with reports of a breaking scandal, company executives deliberately concealed the news from both shareholders and consumers on purpose because they feared the inevitable financial consequences.

6. Both the raw ingredients and distillation technology used by early perfumers significantly influenced the development of chemistry, on which it had an important effect.

7. Although the city of Troy, described by Homer in *The Illiad*, was long believed to be an imaginary city that did not exist, recent excavations have revealed remains consistent with some of the locations depicted in the book.

8. Vietnam became independent from Imperial China in 938 AD following the Battle of Bach Dang River, with consecutive Vietnamese royal dynasties flourishing one after the other as the nation expanded geographically and politically into Southeast Asia.

9. Hydrothermal vents, fissures in a planet's surface from which heated water spurts, are commonly found near active volcanoes as well as areas where tectonic plates diverge.

10. Historically, only a small group of educated elites were taught to write in the past, so written records tend to reflect the assumptions and values of a limited range of individuals.

14. DICTION

Diction errors (also known as usage or "wrong word" errors) generally appear at most once per test, and often they do not appear at all. They are created by switching two similar- or identical-sounding but differently spelled words.

Incorrect:	The work of Portuguese Renaissance painter Gregorio Lopes **insists** mostly of frescoes for monasteries across the Iberian Peninsula.
Correct:	The work of Portuguese Renaissance painter Gregorio Lopes **consists** mostly of frescoes for monasteries across the Iberian Peninsula.

Below is a list of commonly confused words. Pairs that have appeared on recent SATs are marked with asterisk. **Please be aware, however, that like preposition errors, diction errors are often extremely random and cannot be predicted with any degree of confidence.**

Accept vs. Except	Command vs. Commend	Imply vs. Infer
Access vs. Excess	Comprehensive vs. Comprehensible	Incur vs. Occur
Addition vs. Edition	Conscious vs. Conscience	Indeterminate vs. Interminable
Adopt vs. Adapt	Contribute vs. Attribute	Influence vs. Affluence
Advice vs. Advise	Counsel vs. Council	Ingenious vs. Ingenuous
Affect vs. Effect	Contemptuous vs. Contemptible	Lie vs. Lay/Laid vs. Lain
Afflict vs. Inflict	(In)credible vs. (In)credulous	Perspective vs. Prospective
Allude vs. Elude	Desirous vs. Desirable*	Precede vs. Proceed*
Allusion vs. Illusion	Devise vs. Device	Precedent vs. President
Ambivalent vs. Ambiguous	Elicit vs. Illicit	Perpetrate vs. Perpetuate
Anecdote vs. Antidote	Emit vs. Omit	Persecute vs. Prosecute
Appraise vs. Apprise	Ensure vs. Assure	Principal vs. Principle
Assent vs. Ascent	Exhaustive vs. Exhausting	Respective vs. Respectful*
Auditory vs. Audible*	Expandable vs. Expendable	Sensible vs. Sensitive vs. Sensory
Averse vs. Adverse	Explicit vs. Implicit	Simulate vs. Stimulate
Capital vs. Capitol	Flaunt vs. Flout	Supposed to, NOT suppose to*
Censor vs. Censure	Foreboding vs. Forbidding	Than vs. Then
Collaborate vs.	Imminent vs. Eminent*	Visual vs. Visible*
Corroborate*	Implicit vs. Complicit	Would/Could/Should have, NOT of*

Diction Exercises

In the following sentence, identify and correct any diction that appears. Some sentences may not contain an error. (Answers p. 169)

1. To attract perspective students, the university has planned a series of lectures and open houses designed to exhibit its wide variety of academic programs and newly renovated facilities.

2. Since its publication last year, the biography has earned anonymous praise, with everyone from casual readers to established critics agreeing that it is one of the best books of its kind in recent memory.

3. During the trial, the defense attorney argued that the police's repeated questioning of the suspect without a lawyer present represented a clear volition of his client's rights.

4. Large fires, far from destroying forests, can act as catalysts that simulate biodiversity and promote ecological health throughout an ecosystem.

5. When she returned home from the library, Ines was surprised to discover that her wallet was missing because she was not at all conscience of having dropped anything as she walked.

6. The physics professor was awarded the university's top teaching award because of her ability to make a difficult subject unusually comprehensive to her students.

7. Henry wanted to enter his project in the state science fair, but the judges decided that it was not eligible because it failed to meet the criteria laid out in the guidelines for submission.

8. The biologists wore masks as well as gloves during their dissent into the cave because it was believed to be a natural reservoir for several highly infectious diseases.

9. A dog's ears are far more sensory than those of a human: they pick up frequencies at more than twice the range that human ears can perceive.

10. Although the fugitive managed to allude capture for several weeks, he was finally caught after his picture was displayed on national television for several consecutive days.

15. MISCELLANEOUS: ERROR-IDENTIFICATION

The following are common "trick" words and phrases that often sound wrong but that are actually correct.

A means of

There is nothing wrong with this phrase. A lot of test-takers think that it is incorrect because the words *means* seems plural, and of course you can't have the construction *a + plural noun*. In this case, the word *means* is singular, and it's fine.

Long since

This is another construction that the SAT is fond of. Test-takers tend to get tricked because they think it sounds odd, but it's perfectly acceptable. If the following sentence were an SAT question, the answer would be "No error."

> Correct: The ruins of the Roman arena had a desolate atmosphere, abandoned as they were by
> spectators **long since** gone.

"That" as part of a subject

When used to begin a sentence, the phrase *the fact that* is often simply reduced to *that*. Although you may not be familiar with the construction, it is correct.

> Correct: **That** Mark Twain made substantial contributions to nineteenth century literary theory
> should come as no surprise given his importance in the world of letters.

"What" as part of a subject

There is absolutely nothing wrong with starting a sentence with *what*, even if it's not a question. Note that *what*, when used a subject, always takes a singular verb.

> Correct: **What** has been criticized **is** the author's refusal to discuss her work publicly, not the
> content of her novels.

"Whether" as part of a subject

This is yet another construction that many test-takers are unfamiliar with and incorrectly believe is wrong. Again, it's perfectly acceptable, regardless of how odd you may think it sounds. As is true for *what*, *whether* takes a singular verb.

> Correct: **Whether** *The Tale of Genji* was actually written entirely by Murasaki Shikibu **is** unlikely to ever be
> determined unless a major archival discovery is made.

Herself/Himself/Itself

All of these words are correct when used for emphasis. Just make sure that they agree with the noun they emphasize.

Incorrect:	What has been criticized is the author's refusal to discuss her work publicly, not the quality of <u>the writing</u> **herself**.
Correct:	What has been criticized is the author's refusal to discuss her work publicly, not the quality of <u>the writing</u> **itself**.

Alike

The word *alike* tends to throw people off because it sounds like it could be wrong. It's not. It's fine, so ignore it.

Correct:	The media's criticism has been directed at both the company's executives and its shareholders **alike**.

(Al)though + Adjective or Past Participle

Correct:	**Though known** to audiences primarily for his appearances in films such as *Glory*, André Braugher has also appeared in numerous theatrical productions.

People tend to get fooled by this construction because they think it should read, *Though <u>he is known</u> to audiences primarily for his appearances in films such as Glory....* In reality, the sentence is correct either way. The pronoun and verb are optional.

In that

> In that = because

Although the phrase may sound somewhat awkward, there's nothing inherently wrong with it. If it's underlined in the Error-Identification section and creates the correct logical relationship, it's fine.

One of a kind vs. One of its kind

Incorrect:	In 2008, engineers in Geneva completed the Large Hadron Collider, an immense high-energy particle accelerator that is the only **one of a kind** in Europe.
Correct:	In 2008, engineers in Geneva completed the Large Hadron Collider, an immense high-energy particle accelerator that is the only **one of its kind** in Europe.

Since the Large Hadron Collider is not the only particle accelerator in the world, *one of its kind* should be used instead.

Any vs. Any other

Incorrect:	A source of intense fascination for both art historians and museum patrons, Leonardo da Vinci's *Mona Lisa* is perhaps more famous than **any** painting in the world.
Correct:	A source of intense fascination for both art historians and museum patrons, Leonardo da Vinci's *Mona Lisa* is perhaps more famous than **any other** painting in the world.

By saying the *Mona Lisa* is more famous than *any* painting, the first version implies that the *Mona Lisa* is not a painting.

16. ERROR-IDENTIFICATON STRATEGIES

So now that you know pretty much everything there is to know about Error-Identification questions, let's look at how you can use that knowledge to attack the test.

If, after reading a sentence closely several times, you still cannot find an obvious error, don't panic! Instead of simply trying to hear something that sounds wrong, you are now going to work from the information you've been given – the underlined words and phrases – and use it, along with your knowledge of the errors and clues, to very systematically determine whether there is in fact a problem. And if there isn't, you're going to shut your eyes, hope for the best, and just pick option E (although you should probably open your eyes before you fill in the little bubble).

As a general rule, you want to check for the most common errors first: if *its* or *there is* underlined, you should start with that answer choice because there's a very good chance that it's the problem. Otherwise, check the verbs first: *is/are*, *was/were*, and *has/have*, along with any other verbs in the present tense, should be very high on your list – no matter how complicated the sentence might appear. While there are theoretically many possibilities for errors, the reality is that only a handful of errors show up very frequently, and you need to make sure to look out for them. If there isn't a problem with subject-verb agreement, verb tense, or pronoun agreement, there's *already* a reasonable chance that the answer is "No error." One of the things that the SAT tests is the ability to sort through lots of information and figure out which parts of it are actually relevant to the task at hand. It is not in the least unusual to encounter a complex, awkward-sounding, multi-clause sentence, only to have the error turn out to be something as simple as *is*.

Remember: if a particular error is indicated by the structure and/or wording of a sentence, and that error does not appear, the answer is likely to be "No error." So, for example, if a sentence includes a date or time period but no verb error, there's a good chance that nothing is wrong.

While it can be tempting to skip steps and just assume you'll hear the error if there is one, that's usually wishful thinking. SAT sentences are constructed very deliberately to make things that are right sound wrong, and things that are wrong sound right. If you're truly the exception and happen to have a foolproof ear, you can stop right here, but if you're not – a category that includes 99% of test-takers – keep reading.

Example #1

> Writing <u>about</u> scientific matters <u>poses</u> a problem because one
>   A   B
>
> must choose <u>imprecise</u> metaphors that allow <u>you</u> to put new
>   C   D
>
> findings in perspective for non-scientists. <u>No error</u>
>   E

If you can spot the clue (or the error) in the sentence right away, great. But regardless, you can still use this process as a model – or a **paradigm**, to use a favorite SAT word – for what to do when you can't spot the error easily. Choice by choice, we're going to consider the error possibilities by category.

Choice (B):

poses = singular verb, present tense

This is our top error candidate, so we start with it. We have two options: subject-verb agreement or verb tense.

Since subject-verb agreement is the most common error, we start by looking for the subject: *writing*. It's singular, so that's fine. It is, however, separated from the verb by a prepositional phrase that ends with a plural noun (*about scientific matters*), so careful not to get tricked into thinking that *matters* is the subject of *poses*.

Now we move to tense. There's no date or time period, which suggests that this is not a tense question, but just to be sure, we check the other verbs in the sentence: *must* and *allow*. Both are in the present tense, so *poses* is ok.

Choice (A):

writing = gerund

about = preposition

We'll start with the gerund: gerunds get switched with infinitives, so we plug in the infinitive:

> **To write** about scientific matters poses a problem because one must choose imprecise metaphors that allow you to put new findings in perspective for non-scientists.

An infinitive can work as the subject of a sentence, but here, there's no grammatical or stylistic reason (e.g. preserving parallel structure) to use one in place of the gerund. So *writing* is fine.

Now the preposition: *write about* is standard usage, so that's not the problem either.

Choice (C):

imprecise = adjective

Adjectives get switched with adverbs, so we plug in the adverb:

> Writing about science poses a problem because one must choose **imprecisely** metaphors that allow you to put new findings in perspective for non-scientists.

Ick.

Choice (D):

you = pronoun

you gets switched with *one*, so we plug in *one*:

> Writing about science poses a problem because **one** must choose imprecise metaphors that allow **one** to put new findings in perspective for non-scientists.

Bingo! How do we know this is the answer? Because *one* already appears in the sentence, and the pronoun must stay consistent.

Choice (E):

No longer an option.

In case you were wondering, here's the **shortcut:** the pronouns *one* and *you* typically appear in sentences only when one of them is incorrect. So right from the start, (D) is actually the most likely candidate.

Of course you won't have time to pore over every question on the test this way. But training yourself to look systematically at the error options gives you a means of getting out of trouble when you don't spot a problem immediately. Even if you have to slow down a little for one or two questions, you're a whole lot more likely to answer them correctly than you would be if you just guessed. Besides, once you get used to working through sentences like this, the process goes much, much faster. The payoff can also be massive: well over 100 points, and sometimes close to 200.

So let's try another one.

Example #2

> Sumerian cuneiform <u>script</u>, one of the first writing systems,
>   A
> <u>was</u> <u>comprised in</u> symbols carved into soft clay and grew out
> B   C
> of merchants' schemes <u>for keeping</u> accounts. <u>No error</u>
>   D   E

Choice (B):

Again, we're going to start with the underlined verb.

> *was* = singular verb, simple past

Subject-Verb Agreement: What's the subject? *Script*, which is singular. So we're ok.

Tense: even if you don't know who the Sumerians were, you have a clue (*one of the first writing systems*) that suggests we're talking about something that happened a pretty long time ago. So simple past is fine.

Choice (A):

> *script* = noun

Nouns are usually right, so we're going to ignore it for the time being.

Choice (C):

> *in* = preposition

This is tricky. Is the phrase *comprised in*, or is there some other preposition that should be used?

If you don't know, leave it.

Choice (D):

> *for keeping* = preposition + gerund

Gerunds get switched with infinitives, so plug in the infinitive:

> Sumerian cuneiform script, one of the first writing systems, was comprised in symbols carved into soft clay and grew out of merchants' schemes **to keep** accounts.

It's ok, but *for keeping* sounds better. Which leaves us with (C) and (E). Is it weird, or is it wrong?

In this case, it's wrong (the phrase is *comprised of*), but even if you didn't know that, you could get it down to two choices. And whenever you're left with a preposition option and (E), you should in fact think about how you'd say the phrase. If your ear is usually reliable and what you would say doesn't match, chances are the preposition is incorrect. If you have absolutely no idea and aren't trying for a 700+ score, you're probably better of leaving it blank.

One more.

Example #3

Let's pretend that this is question #27 of the first Writing section (third to last Error-Identification question). Right away, that gives us some clues as to what kind of error, if any, is likely to appear. Our likeliest categories are:

- Faulty comparison
- Subject-verb agreement (involving a prepositional phrase)
- Pronoun-antecedent
- Preposition/idiom
- No error

Like Aesop's fables, <u>the Brothers Grimm</u> used talking animals to
              A
expose human vices and in <u>doing so</u> challenged <u>rigid</u>
                        B   C
boundaries between humans <u>and</u> other species. <u>No error</u>
                        D   E

We're going to approach this question a little differently from how we approached the previous one. First, there are three options we can eliminate almost immediately:

Choice (B):

The phrase *doing so* is generally correct. The problem usually is with the phrase *doing it*. So for the moment, we're going to assume that it's ok.

Choice (C):

rigid = adjective

The only other option is the adverb, *rigidly*, which clearly doesn't work when we plug it in.

Choice D:

and is correctly paired with *between*, so that can't be the answer.

Choice (A):

We know that a faulty comparison is likely, and the word *like* provides a big clue because it tells us right away that two things are being compared. What's being compared to what?

Aesop's fables = things   vs.   *The Brothers Grimm* = people

So the sentence should correctly read:

> Like Aesop's fables, **those of** the Brothers Grimm used talking animals to expose human vices and in doing so challenged rigid boundaries between humans and other species.

So now you try it. **(Answers are on p. 169)**

Practice #1

Blessed <u>with</u> an <u>exceptional</u> rugged natural landscape,
     A   B
New Zealand <u>has drawn</u> thrill-seeking athletes in search
              C
<u>of</u> adventure for decades. <u>No error</u>
D   E

Clues (if any):

And if you're still not sure:

Choice (A)

Category: _____

Choice (B)

Category: _____

Choice (C)

Category: _____

Choice (D)

Category: _____

Answer:

Practice #2

Franz Kafka's novel *The Trial* <u>opens with</u> the unexplained
A

arrest <u>of</u> Josef K. by a <u>mysterious</u> organization that runs
   B   C

<u>their</u> courts outside the normal criminal-justice system.
 D

<u>No error</u>
   E

Clues (if any):

And if you're still not sure:

Choice (A)

Category: _____

Choice (B)

Category: _____

Choice (C)

Category: _____

Choice (D)

Category: _____

Answer:

Practice #3

Hidden in a trunk for nearly seventy years <u>were</u> a
A

camera and <u>nearly</u> a thousand photographic negatives
B

<u>given to</u> former Mexican ambassador Francisco Aguilar
C

Gonzalez <u>for</u> safekeeping. <u>No error</u>
D   E

Clues (if any):

And if you're still not sure:

Choice (A)

Category: _____

Choice (B)

Category: _____

Choice (C)

Category: _____

Choice (D)

Category: _____

Answer:

Error-Identification Test

1. *The Last Five years*, a musical <u>written by</u> Jason
                                      A
   Robert Brown, premiered <u>in</u> Chicago in 2001 and
                            B
   <u>being produced</u> numerous times <u>both</u> in the
   C   D
   United States and internationally. <u>No error</u>
                                          E

2. <u>Among</u> the many reasons healthcare
   A
   professionals <u>choose</u> jobs that require travel <u>are</u>
                 B   C
   higher pay, professional growth and development,

   and <u>to have</u> personal adventures. <u>No error</u>
       D   E

3. The tower of London, which <u>lies</u> within the
                                A
   Borough of Tower Hamlets, <u>are</u> separated from
                             B
   the city <u>itself</u> by a stretch of <u>open</u> space. <u>No error</u>
            C   D   E

4. Originally a common breakfast eaten by farmers

   <u>which</u> lived in the canton of Bern, rösti <u>is</u> today
   A   B
   <u>considered</u> the unofficial national dish <u>of</u>
   C   D
   Switzerland. <u>No error</u>
                E

5. The Australian frilled lizard <u>responds to</u> attacks
                                  A
   <u>by</u> unfurling the colorful skin flap that encircles
   B
   <u>its</u> head, but if all else fails it will scoot <u>nimble</u> up
   C   D
   the nearest tree. <u>No error</u>
                     E

6. Sofia Tolstoy, <u>the wife of</u> Russian author
                  A
   Leo Tolstoy, was a woman <u>of strength</u> and
                            B
   spirit <u>who understood</u> the high price she <u>will pay</u>
          C   D
   to live next to one of the greatest writers in

   history. <u>No error</u>
            E

7. James Watson and Francis Crick <u>were</u> renowned
                                   A
   as <u>a scientist</u> because <u>they</u> discovered the DNA
      B   C
   triple helix and in 1962 were <u>awarded</u> the Nobel
                                 D
   Prize in Medicine. <u>No error</u>
                      E

8. Among nations known <u>for producing</u>
                        A
   exceptional chess players, neither China <u>or</u> Russia
                                            B
   can compete with Armenia for the <u>sheer number</u> of
                                    C
   grandmasters <u>it has produced</u>. <u>No error</u>
                D   E

9. Humor is a far <u>more subtler</u> process <u>than</u> a
                  A   B
   primeval pleasure such as <u>eating</u>, but it is just as
                             C
   much <u>tied to</u> the inner complexity of the brain.
        D
   <u>No error</u>
   E

10. Frequently <u>dismissed as</u> a vice, gossip is in fact
               A
    a <u>means of</u> creating alliances <u>and</u> friendships
      B   C
    among <u>members of</u> groups. <u>No error</u>
          D   E

11. The secret of the Mona Lisa's enigmatic smile

   is a matter of which cells in the retina pick up the
   ‎   A   B   C
   image and how it channels the information to the
   ‎   D
   brain. No error
   ‎   E

12. Located on the outskirts of Lincoln National
   ‎ A
   Forest in New Mexico, White Oaks had become a
   ‎   B
   boomtown after silver and gold were discovered
   ‎   C
   in the nearby Jicarilla Mountains in 1879.
   ‎   D
   No error
   ‎ E

13. The Ethiopian wolf, the only species of wolf

   native in Africa, can be identified by its distinctive
   ‎   A   B   C
   red coat and black-and-white tail. No error
   ‎   D   E

14. Far from eliminating war, the new diplomatic
   ‎ A
   system instituted in Europe during the early
   ‎   B
   nineteenth century simply changed the reasons

   to fight and the methods of combat. No error
   ‎ C   D   E

15. With genes that are virtually identical to

   humans, Neanderthals can offer many insights into
   ‎ A   B   C
   the evolution and development of the modern
   ‎   D
   brain. No error
   ‎   E

16. The popularity of games such as cricket and

   squash in former English colonies are often
   ‎   A
   attributed to the lingering influence of British
   ‎ B   C   D
   culture. No error
   ‎   E

17. Central to the emergence of women as a major
   ‎ A
   force in American political life was the rise of the
   ‎ B   C
   female career politician determined to devote her
   ‎   D
   life to public service. No error
   ‎   E

Answers can be found on page 169.

17. FIXING SENTENCES: INTRODUCTION AND RULES FOR CHOOSING ANSWERS

Although most of the errors that appear in the Error-Identification section appear in Fixing Sentences as well, there are also some important differences. While the former often contains errors that revolve around misuse of individual words and parts of speech (e.g. verbs, pronouns, adjectives, prepositions), the latter is more concerned with errors in the structure of the sentences themselves. Fixing Sentences tests your ability to distinguish full sentences from sentence fragments and to distinguish clear and concise phrasings from long and awkward ones. The major concepts that are covered primarily in Fixing Sentence are as follows:

1) Sentences and Fragments

2) Commas and Semicolons

3) Gerunds and Wordiness

4) Dangling Modifiers

5) Active vs. Passive Voice

6) "Phrase" Parallel Structure

Subject-Verb Agreement, Pronoun-Antecedent, Verb Tense and Form, "List" Parallel Structure, Noun Agreement, Faulty Comparisons, Conjunctions, and Word Pairs are also tested, but to a somewhat lesser extent than in the Error-Identification section.

Relative Pronoun, Redundancy, and Preposition errors appear as well, but rarely.

The following errors do not generally appear in Fixing Sentences:

-Pronoun Case
-Double Negatives/Double Positives
-Comparatives vs. Superlatives
-Adjectives vs. Adverbs
-Diction

Rules for Choosing Answers

While it is always most effective to identify and correct errors before looking at the answers, working this way can be an exercise in frustration if you do not know quite what you are looking for or are unsure of how to fix it. If you do choose to look at the answers, there are three general rules that should dictate your approach to eliminating choices.

1) Shorter is Better

Always check answers in order of length, starting with the shortest one. Since you are being tested on your ability to eliminate wordiness, it is logical that more concise answers are more likely to be correct.

When you are faced with two grammatically correct answers that express the same essential information, the shorter one will always be right.

2) Gerunds (-ING words), especially BEING = BAD

Gerunds create sentence fragments and awkwardness. In the vast majority of cases that require you to choose between a conjugated verb and a gerund, the conjugated verb will be correct.

In general, you should only choose a gerund in the following cases:

   -It is necessary to preserve parallel structure.

   -It is required by standard usage.

   -It is required to create the cleanest, clearest, and most concise version of a sentence.

Furthermore, you should automatically eliminate any answer that contains the word *being*, unless it is absolutely, incontrovertibly necessary (not the case 98% of the time).

3) Passive Voice = BAD

   Active = The politician **gave** a speech.

   Passive = A speech **was given** by the politician.

The passive version is unnecessarily wordy. You should automatically eliminate any answer containing this construction unless the sentence does not make sense without it.

18. SENTENCES AND FRAGMENTS

Every sentence must contain two elements: a subject and a verb that corresponds to it. A sentence can consist of only one word (*Go!* is a sentence because the subject, *you*, is implied), or of many complex clauses, but provided that it contains a subject and a verb, it is considered to be grammatically complete – *regardless of whether it makes logical sense outside of any context.*

Any phrase that lacks a subject (noun or pronoun) and a main verb that corresponds to it cannot be a sentence. Instead, it is a fragment.

Fixing Sentences answer choices that contain fragments are always incorrect.

In Fixing Sentences, there are two general types of fragments:

    1) Gerunds replace verbs

    2) Relative clause errors

Gerunds Replace Verbs

As described on p. 21, gerunds are formed by adding –ING to verbs (e.g. to run → running; to go → going).

Gerunds are sneaky: they look like verbs but act like nouns. What this means, practically speaking, is that a clause containing only a gerund cannot be a sentence. Instead, it is a fragment.

    Fragment: George C. Williams **being** one of the most important recent thinkers in the field of evolutionary biology.

To turn a fragment containing a gerund into a sentence, simply replace the gerund with a conjugated verb:

    Sentence: George C. Williams **was** one of the most important recent thinkers in the field of evolutionary biology.

Important: *being* is the most frequently tested gerund on the SAT.

The conjugated forms of it are as follows:

    Present: is/are

    Past: was/were

Relative Clause Errors

A sentence that contains a relative clause must always contain a main verb that corresponds to the subject. Relative clauses can be either essential or non-essential.

Non-essential relative clauses with "which" or "who(se)"

Fragment: George C. Williams, who was one of the most important thinkers in the field of
              evolutionary biology.

In the above fragment, the construction *comma + who* suggests that a non-essential clause is beginning, but there is never a second comma – the sentence ends without a resolution.

The only verb (*was*) that appears in the sentence is part of the relative clause begun by the relative pronoun *who*, not part of the main clause begun by the subject (*George C. Williams*).

The fastest and easiest way to turn this fragment into a sentence is to remove the comma and the relative pronoun, thereby eliminating the relative clause and making the entire sentence into a single main clause.

Sentence: George C. Williams was one of the most important thinkers in the field of
              evolutionary biology.

Now the verb *was* clearly belongs to the subject.

Many of the fragments that appear in Fixing Sentences will be slightly longer, however:

Fragment: George C. Williams, who was one of the most important thinkers in evolutionary
              biology, and who made a number of lasting contributions to his field.

In the above sentence, we can identify what appears to be a non-essential clause (*who was…biology*) because it begins with *who* and is surrounded by commas. If we cross it out, however, we are left with:

Fragment: George C. Williams…**and who made** a number of lasting contributions to his field.

Clearly this is not a sentence. Making it into a sentence, however, is relatively simple: since the first word after the end of a non-essential clause is typically a verb, we can cross out all the excess words before the verb. This leaves us with:

Sentence: George C. Williams…~~and who~~ made a number of lasting contributions to his field.

With the elimination of those two words, the fragment suddenly becomes a sentence. When we plug the non-essential clause back in, we get something much clearer:

Sentence: George C. Williams, who was one of the most important thinkers in evolutionary
              biology, **made** a number of lasting contributions to his field.

Another possible solution is to remove the non-essential clause entirely.

Sentence: George C. Williams **was** one of the most important thinkers in the field of evolutionary
              biology and made a number of lasting contributions to his field.

This is one of the most common Fixing Sentences errors. A version of it nearly always appears at least once per section, often in the first three or four questions.

To sum up:

The easiest way to attack sentences like this is to see if there is a verb immediately following a non-essential clause. If there is not, the sentence is virtually always incorrect. (The only exception would be something along the lines of: *George C. Williams, who was one of the most important recent American thinkers in evolutionary biology, also made a number of lasting contributions to his field*, because the sentence still makes sense if the non-essential clause is eliminated.)

Cross out everything after the second comma and before the verb, and the sentence that remains will nearly always match the correct answer choice.

Again:

Fragment:	Mobile robot technology, which has historically been used by both the military and the police, and it is now becoming widespread at businesses and hotels.
Reduce:	Mobile robot technology, ~~which has historically been used by both the military and the police,~~ and it is now becoming widespread at businesses and hotels.
Cross Out:	Mobile robot technology…~~and it~~ is now becoming widespread at businesses and hotels.
Sentence:	Mobile robot technology, which has historically been used by both the military and the police, is now becoming widespread at businesses and hotels.

Important: occasionally you will be asked to fix the beginning of a non-essential clause rather than the end.

Fragment:	Mobile robot technology has historically been used by both the military and the police, is now becoming widespread at businesses and hotels.

Sentences like these can be tricky because the beginning looks fine; it's the end that appears to need fixing. In cases such as these, however, the second comma followed by a verb is your clue that a non-essential clause needs to be created in order to correct the sentence.

Sentence:	Mobile robot technology**, which has** historically been used by both the military and the police, is now becoming widespread at businesses and hotels.

Essential relative clauses with "that"

Clauses beginning with the relative pronoun *that* function exactly like those beginning with *which* or *who(se)*, even though they are essential (or **restrictive**) and do not require commas to be placed around them.

Fragment:	The mobile robot technology that has historically been used by both the military and the police and that is now becoming widespread at businesses and hotels.
Cross out:	The mobile robot technology that has historically been used by both the military and the police ~~and that~~ is now becoming widespread at businesses and hotels.
Sentence:	The mobile robot technology that has historically been used by both the military and the police is now becoming widespread at businesses and hotels.

94

Important: answer choices that contain properly used non-essential clauses are virtually always correct.

The SAT will sometimes include sentences with multiple non-essential clauses. Although such sentences may seem unnecessarily complex and awkward to you, they are virtually guaranteed to be correct in the absence of any other error.

Correct: Cleopatra, the last of the pharaohs and presumably the only one fluent in the common speech, probably spoke only Greek, the language of the ruling class, in private.

The sentence contains two non-essential clauses, which can be crossed out as follows:

Correct: Cleopatra, ~~the last of the pharaohs and presumably the only one fluent in the common speech,~~ probably spoke only Greek, ~~the language of the ruling class,~~ in private.

Because the sentence that makes perfect grammatical sense (*Cleopatra probably spoke only Greek in private*), the

ETS will also frequently include correct sentences with short non-essential clauses or phrases in unexpected places because they know that many test-takers are unaccustomed to such constructions. For example:

Correct: A planet capable of harboring life, astronomers think, may be identified sometime within the next decade.

Correct: St. Petersburg is a charming, if frigid, city to visit during the wintertime.

Do not be fooled by the unexpected syntax. Both of these sentences are perfectly fine as is. And yes, people do actually write this way sometimes!

Sentence and Fragment Exercises

Label each of the following phrases as either a sentence or a fragment. Rewrite all fragments as sentences. (Answers p. 170, Official Guide question list p. 147)

1. Shirley Jackson, best known for her shocking short story "The Lottery," and who was born in San Francisco in 1916.

2. The tenth legion, among the oldest in the imperial Roman army, originally fought on horseback under Caesar's command.

3. The pyramids of ancient Egypt, intended to be monuments to the Pharaohs' greatness and were built with the help of great armies of slaves.

4. The Red Belt was one of several colored belts used in some martial arts to denote a practitioner's skill level and rank, originated in Japan and Korea.

5. The plan to overhaul the country's higher education system being a model for moving other desperately needed projects forward.

6. Patients who receive anesthesia during surgery are put into a semi-comatose state, not, as many people assume, a deep state of sleep.

7. Recent findings from research on moose, which have suggested that arthritis in human beings may be linked in part to nutritional deficits.

8. A new study reporting that the physical differences among dog breeds are determined by variations in only about seven genetic regions.

9. George Barr McCutcheon, a popular novelist and playwright, and he is best known for the series of novels set in Graustark, a fictional Eastern European country.

10. Forensic biology is the application of biology to law enforcement, has been used to identify illegal products from endangered species and investigate bird collisions with wind turbines.

11. Human computers, who once performed basic numerical analysis for laboratories, and they were behind the calculations for everything from the first accurate prediction of the return of Halley's Comet to the success of the Manhattan Project.

12. Nicollet Island, an island in the Mississippi River just north of Minneapolis, and which was named after cartographer Joseph Nicollet.

13. Malba Tahan, who was a fictitious Persian scholar and who was the pen name created by Brazilian author Júlio César de Mello e Souza.

14. The Rochester International Jazz Festival taking place in June of each year and typically attracts more than 100,000 fans from towns across upstate New York.

15. Although Rodin purposely omitted crucial elements such as arms from his sculptures, his consistent use of the human figure attesting to his respect for artistic tradition.

16. Brick nog, a commonly used construction technique in which one width of bricks is used to fill the vacancies in a wooden frame.

17. The unusually large size of the komodo dragon, the largest species of lizard, which has been attributed to its ancient ancestor, the immense varanid lizard.

18. One of the most popular ballets, *Swan Lake*, which was fashioned from Russian folk tales, telling the story of Odette, a princess turned into a swan by an evil sorcerer's curse.

19. Simone Fortini, a postmodern choreographer who was born in Italy but moved to the United States at a young age, rapidly became known for a style of dancing based on improvisation and everyday movements.

20. Pheidon, a king of the Greek city Argos during the seventh century B.C., and he ruled during a time when monarchs were figureheads with little genuine power.

21. Batsford Arboretum, a 55-acre garden that contains Great Britain's largest collection of Japanese cherry trees and it is open daily to the public for most of the year.

19. FIXING COMMA SPLICES: COMMAS, *FANBOYS*, AND SEMICOLONS

Commas and semicolons are two of the most commonly tested concepts in Fixing Sentences. They are tested only in relation to combining full sentences (or **independent clauses**) with one another.

A **comma splice** is created when a comma is used to separate two independent clauses (complete sentences). Comma splices are always wrong – no exceptions – and they are *everywhere* in Fixing Sentences. Not only does virtually every section contain at least one question that tests them directly, but many incorrect answers to questions testing *other* concepts contain them as well.

Let us consider the following two clauses:

Clause #1:   Both the Parthenon and the Pantheon are temples to the deities of the people who built them.

Clause #2:   The Parthenon was built by the Greeks while the Pantheon was constructed by the Romans.

If we want to join those two clauses to create a single sentence, we cannot place **only** a comma between them.

Comma Splice: Both the Parthenon and the Pantheon are temples to the deities of the people who built **them, the** Parthenon was built by the Greeks while the Pantheon was constructed by the Romans.

The SAT tests your ability to recognize four principal ways of fixing comma splices:

1) Comma + Coordinating (FANBOYS) Conjunction

2) Dependent Clause

3) Semicolon Only

4) Semicolon + Conjunctive Adverb

A. Comma + Coordinating (FANBOYS) Conjunction

There are seven coordinating conjunctions, known by the acronym FANBOYS:

For
And
Nor
But
Or
Yet
So

FANBOYS conjunctions can be used to join independent clauses, and they must always come after a comma when they are employed in this way. Without a comma, a sentence that uses a FANBOYS conjunction to join two independent clauses is technically a run-on sentence, regardless of how short it is.

Run-On:	Both the Parthenon and the Pantheon are temples to the deities of the people who built **them but** the Parthenon was built by the Greeks while the Pantheon was constructed by the Romans.
Correct:	Both the Parthenon and the Pantheon are temples to the deities of the people who built **them, but** the Parthenon was built by the Greeks while the Pantheon was constructed by the Romans.

B. Dependent Clause

You can also fix a comma splice by changing one of the **independent clauses** into a **dependent clause**. One way to create a dependent clause is to add a **subordinating conjunction** such as *(al)though*, *when*, or *because* to the start of one of the clauses.

Correct:	**Although** both the Parthenon and the Pantheon are temples to the deities of the people who built **them, the** Parthenon was built by the Greeks while the Pantheon was constructed by the Romans.

Because the subordinating conjunction *although* makes the first clause dependent, the comma between the two clauses no longer forms a comma splice and is entirely acceptable.

Also: contrary to what you may have learned, you can begin a sentence with *because*, provided that the sentence contains a main (independent) clause in addition to the clause begun by *because*.

Incorrect:	Because the Pantheon has been preserved intact for nearly eighteen centuries.
Correct:	Because the Pantheon has been preserved intact for nearly eighteen centuries, **thousands of tourists flock to visit it each year**.

But: any answer choice that contains the construction *comma + because* is incorrect.

Incorrect:	Thousands of tourists flock to visit the Pantheon each **year, because** it has been preserved intact for nearly eighteen centuries.
Correct:	Thousands of tourists flock to visit the Pantheon each **year because** it has been preserved intact for nearly eighteen centuries.

Sometimes it is also possible to create a dependent clause by changing the first clause into a **participial phrase**.

Incorrect:	**Augustus Caesar decided** to undertake a program of construction in the aftermath of the Battle of Actium, he commissioned the Pantheon as a monument to all the deities of Rome.
Correct:	**Having decided** to undertake a program of construction in the aftermath of the Battle of Actium, Augustus Caesar commissioned the Pantheon as a monument to all the deities of Rome.

Note: In the correct version of the sentence, the word *having* is a participle rather than a gerund and thus does not violate the "no gerund" rule. (See Chapter 20 on p. 110 for more information.)

C. Semicolon

A semicolon functions almost exactly like a period: it is used to separate two independent clauses. Although in real life it is sometimes acceptable to place a semicolon before a FANBOYS conjunction in order to break up a very long sentence, **the College Board always considers it incorrect to place a FANBOYS conjunction after a semicolon.**

Incorrect:	Both the Parthenon and the Pantheon are temples to the deities of the people who built **them; but** the Parthenon was built by the Greeks while the Pantheon was constructed by the Romans.
Correct:	Both the Parthenon and the Pantheon are temples to the deities of the people who built **them; the** Parthenon was built by the Greeks while the Pantheon was constructed by the Romans.

Although the two clauses express contrasting ideas, it is perfectly correct to join them with only a semicolon. It is helpful to include a conjunction such as *but* or *however* to make the relationship between the clauses immediately clear to the reader, but the absence of a conjunction is not in itself problematic. On the SAT, your goal must be to find the answer that corrects the actual grammatical error; if there is another option that expresses the relationship between the clauses more clearly but creates a new problem, as in the first version of the sentence above, that option will never be correct.

D. Semicolon + Conjunctive Adverb

Place a semicolon, not a comma or a period, before the following five **conjunctive adverbs** when they are used to begin a clause:

However

Therefore

Moreover

Consequently

Nevertheless

Incorrect:	Both the Parthenon and the Pantheon are temples to the deities of the people who built **them, however,** the Parthenon was built by the Greeks while the Pantheon was constructed by the Romans.
Correct:	Both the Parthenon and the Pantheon are temples to the deities of the people who built **them; however,** the Parthenon was built by the Greeks while the Pantheon was constructed by the Romans.

But: when these transitions appear alone in the middle of a clause, they should be surrounded by commas.

Correct: Both the Parthenon and the Pantheon are temples to the deities of the people who built **them; the Parthenon, however,** was built by the Greeks while the Pantheon was constructed by the Romans.

Important: a properly used semicolon very often – but not always – indicates a correct answer. When you recognize that a question is testing comma splices, you should check any answers containing semicolons <u>first</u>.

FANBOYS Conjunction + Verb = No Comma

When using a FANBOYS conjunction to join two independent clauses with the same subject, do not use a comma if the subject is not repeated in the second clause. If you find it too confusing to think about subjects and clauses, simply look at the word **after** the FANBOYS conjunction – if it is a verb, do not use a comma. Compare the following:

Correct: The Pantheon was constructed by the **Romans, but it was** strongly influenced by structures built centuries earlier by the Greeks.

Incorrect: The Pantheon was constructed by the **Romans, but was** strongly influenced by structures built centuries earlier by the Greeks.

Correct: The Pantheon was constructed by the **Romans but was** strongly influenced by structures built centuries earlier by the Greeks.

In the second and third versions of the sentence, the subject, *it*, is not repeated in the second clause. As a result, that clause is dependent, and no comma should be placed before the FANBOYS conjunction *but*.

Important: Fixing Sentences questions that test comma and semicolon usage generally test conjunctions/logical relationships as well. Not only are you responsible for finding the answer that fixes the comma splice but you are also responsible for finding the answer that creates the correct logical relationship. **An answer choice can thus be both grammatically correct and wrong.**

For example:

Woven baskets were at one time used simply for storage and transportation of <u>goods, they are</u> primarily made for decorative purposes today.

(A) goods, they are
(B) goods, these are
(C) goods, and they are
(D) goods; however, they are
(E) goods, this is

The original version of the sentence has all the classic features of a comma splice question: it contains two clauses, both of which are independent and the second of which renames the subject, *baskets*, with the plural pronoun *they*. The comma between the two clauses thus creates a comma splice, so we must find the option that fixes that error.

Looking at the answer choices, we can notice that in addition to (A), choices (B) and (E) also contain the construction *comma + pronoun*, suggesting that they also contain comma splices (they do). We can therefore eliminate them immediately, leaving us with only two choices to consider carefully. Both (C) and (D) are grammatically correct: one fixes the comma splice with *comma + FANBOYS*, while the other uses *semicolon + however*. The difference is that (D) correctly indicates that the two clauses express two contrasting ideas, while (C) does not. So even though (C) fixes the grammatical error, it is not correct.

Although comma splices may look like a punctuation problem, they are more often a grammar problem. When people have difficulty identifying commas splices, it is often not because they do not understand the "no comma between two independent clauses rule" but rather because they cannot always tell when clauses are independent.

Is it a Sentence?

Try this little quiz. For each of the following sentences, circle "independent" if the clause can stand on its own as a full sentence, or "dependent" if it cannot. Answers are on p. 171.

1. Three versions of the painting are on display in the museum

    Independent   Dependent

2. Three versions of it are on display in the museum

    Independent   Dependent

3. They are on display in the museum

    Independent   Dependent

4. They are on display in the museum today

    Independent   Dependent

5. Today they are on display in the museum

    Independent   Dependent

6. Many are currently on display in the museum

    Independent   Dependent

7. Three of them are now on display in the museum

    Independent   Dependent

8. Three of which are now on display in the museum

    Independent   Dependent

9. Several are now on display there

    Independent   Dependent

10. Several of whom have visited the museum

    Independent   Dependent

If you answered all of the questions **both** correctly and confidently, you can skip the next section and go directly to the exercise on p. 108. If you got any questions wrong, or if you got all of them right but weren't certain about some of the answers, you should read the next section.

Common Problems in Recognizing Independent Clauses

There are typically two major factors responsible for the confusion that people experience when trying to distinguish between independent and dependent clauses:

1) Adverbs

2) Pronouns

A. Adverbs and Comma Splices

As discussed in Chapter 3, adverbs modify verbs and are usually created by adding *–ly* onto the ends of adjectives (e.g. *slow* → *slowly*, *bright* → *brightly*). That is true, but it is not the whole story. Another kind of adverb, **adverbs of time** indicate when events occurred; sometimes they end in *–ly*, and sometimes they do not. Common examples:

Today	First	Later	Sometimes	Yesterday
Now	Next	Still	Often	Tomorrow
Currently	Then	Last/Finally	Always	Never

If you think this is staring to sound complicated, don't worry! It's actually very simple. **The only thing you need to know is that the addition of one of these adverbs to a sentence has no effect whatsoever, regardless of where the adverb is placed.** A sentence with an adverb added to the beginning, middle, or end is still a complete sentence.

Sentence:	Three versions of the work hang in Norwegian museums.
Beginning:	**Currently**, three versions of the work hang in Norwegian museums.
Middle:	Three versions of the work **now** hang in Norwegian museums.
End:	Three versions of the work hang in Norwegian museums **today**.

Each of these versions is still a grammatically complete sentence. Although the placement of the adverb in the second example may strike you as odd, the construction is perfectly acceptable and does not affect the sentence.

Because the above clauses are independent, they can only be joined to another complete sentence with a semicolon or *comma* + *FANBOYS*. Using a comma alone would create a comma splice.

Comma Splice:	Edvard Munch created four versions of his iconic painting **"The Scream,"** **currently**, **three versions** of the work hang in Norwegian museums.
Correct:	Edvard Munch created four versions of his iconic painting **"The Scream;"** **currently**, **three versions** of the work hang in Norwegian museums.
Comma Splice:	Edvard Munch created four versions of his iconic painting **"The Scream,"** **three versions** of the work **now** hang in Norwegian museums.
Correct:	Edvard Munch created four versions of his iconic painting **"The Scream;"** **three versions** of the work **now** hang in Norwegian museums.
Comma Splice:	Edvard Munch created four versions of his iconic painting **"The Scream,"** **three versions** of the work hang in Norwegian museums **today**.
Correct:	Edvard Munch created four versions of his iconic painting **"The Scream;"** **three versions** of the work hang in Norwegian museums **today**.

B. Pronouns and Comma Splices

The second common point of confusion about independent clauses involves pronouns. As discussed in Chapter Two, pronouns are words such as *it, they,* and *she* that are used to replace nouns. The chart below lists some common pronouns, all of which are fair game for comma splice questions on the SAT.

Singular	Plural	Singular and Plural
It One She/He This That Each None Any	They Those These Others Some Several Many Most All The majority Numbers larger than one	(N)either There

Shortcut: The construction *comma + pronoun* often signals a comma splice. When you see an answer choice containing that construction, you should automatically be suspicious.

Replacing nouns with pronouns

The most important thing to understand about pronouns is that, like adverbs, they have no effect on whether a clause is independent or dependent. They are simply used to avoid repeating nouns and making sentences unnecessarily wordy and awkward. For example, consider the following version of this sentence:

Sentence: **The tomato** was consumed only in South America for the first thousand years of its existence, but **the tomato** now plays a prominent role in the soups, stews, and sauces of many different cuisines around the world.

The repetition of the subject, *the tomato,* in the second clause probably seems very awkward. The sentence would read much more smoothly if we replaced the noun *the tomato* in the second clause with the pronoun *it*:

Sentence: **The tomato** was consumed only in South America for the first thousand years of its existence, but **it** now plays a prominent role in the soups, stews, and sauces of many different cuisines around the world.

That version sounds a lot better, right? The important thing to understand, however, is that there is no grammatical difference between this version and the first version. The sentence is still composed of two independent clauses; the fact that the second clause now begins with a pronoun and would not make sense out of context changes nothing. If we were to separate the two clauses with only a comma, we would have – you guessed it – a comma splice:

Comma Splice: **The tomato** was consumed only in South America for the first thousand years of its existence, **it** now plays a prominent role in the soups, stews, and sauces of many different cuisines around the world.

If we really wanted to get fancy, we could even replace the noun *tomato* with a pronoun in the first clause:

Sentence: **It** was consumed only in South America for the first thousand years of its existence, but **the tomato** now plays a prominent role in the soups, stews, and sauces of many different cuisines around the world.

Again, we cannot place a comma between the two clauses without creating a comma splice:

Comma Splice: **It** was consumed only in South America for the first thousand years of its existence, **the tomato** now plays a prominent role in the soups, stews, and sauces of many different cuisines around the world.

One more example:

Clause #1:   The ramparts in Old Quebec are the only remaining fortified city walls that still exist in the Americas north of Mexico.

Clause #2:   The ramparts were constructed in Old Quebec by French settlers during the early seventeenth century.

Now we're going to replace some of the nouns in clause #2 with pronouns to avoid repetition:

With Pronouns: **They** were constructed **there** by French settlers during the early seventeenth century.

Again, in context of the first sentence, the second sentence makes sense — we know that *they*, the subject, must refer to the ramparts, and that *there* must refer to Old Quebec. Out of context, however, it's unclear what those pronouns refer to. The clause does not tell us *what* was constructed by French settlers, or *where* it was constructed.

This is where a lot of people run into trouble: they incorrectly assume that because the clause's *meaning* is not entirely clear out of context, the clause cannot actually stand on its own *grammatically* as a complete sentence.

The clause does, however, have a subject (the pronoun *they*) and a main verb that corresponds to it (*were*), so it **can** actually stand on its own as a sentence — and must follow a semicolon or *comma* + *FANBOYS*. The fact that it now includes pronouns rather than nouns is entirely irrelevant.

Comma Splice: The ramparts in Old Quebec are the only remaining fortified city walls that still exist in the Americas north of Mexico, **they** were constructed **there** by French settlers during the early seventeenth century.

Correct: The ramparts in Old Quebec are the only remaining fortified city walls that still exist in the Americas north of Mexico; **they** were constructed **there** by French settlers during the early seventeenth century.

Alternately, it is sometimes possible to correct a comma splice by turning the second clause into a dependent clause beginning with *which* or *who*.

Incorrect: Ownership of the Arctic is governed by the United Nations Convention of the Law of the **Sea, it** gives Arctic nations an exclusive economic zone that extends 200 nautical miles from land.

Correct: Ownership of the Arctic is governed by the United Nations Convention of the Law of the **Sea, which** gives Arctic nations an exclusive economic zone that extends 200 nautical miles from land.

"Group" Pronouns

An additional point of confusion often involves **indefinite** or **"group"** pronouns such as *some, several, few, many,* and *others.* These pronouns can be used to begin clauses in two different ways, one of which creates a comma splice and the other of which does not.

Subject pronoun = comma splice

In this usage, the pronoun simply acts as a subject and is used to replace a noun. It is often followed by the phrase *of them,* but it can be used by itself as well.

Sentence:	Several of them have already been put into effect.
Sentence:	Several have already been put into effect.

Taken out of any context, the above examples don't make much sense, nor do they provide any real information. It is also likely that the second one sounds very strange to you. You might even be wondering whether it's really ok to use *several* that way, without a noun afterward (it's absolutely fine). Regardless of how odd you find these examples, however, they are still sentences because they contain a subject (*several*) and a verb (*have been*) that corresponds to it.

Comma Splice:	The manufacturing company has created an advisory board to oversee the implementation of the new safety **regulations, several of them** have already been put into effect.
Comma Splice:	The manufacturing company has created an advisory board to oversee the implementation of the new safety **regulations, several** have already been put into effect.

In order to fix the sentences on the previous page, it is necessary to replace the comma with either a semicolon or *comma + FANBOYS.*

Correct:	The manufacturing company has created an advisory board to oversee the implementation of new safety **regulations; several (of them)** have already been put into effect.
Correct:	The manufacturing company has created an advisory board to oversee the implementation of the new safety **regulations, and several (of them)** have already been put into effect.

Pronoun + "of which" or "of whom" = no comma splice

When an indefinite pronoun is followed by *of which* or *of whom,* it becomes part of a **dependent clause** and can correctly be separated from an independent clause by only a comma. A semicolon or *comma + FANBOYS* should **not** be used.

Incorrect:	The manufacturing company has created an advisory board to oversee the implementation of the new safety **regulations; several of which** have already been put into effect.
Incorrect:	The manufacturing company has created an advisory board of outside **experts, and many of whom** are nationally recognized in their fields.

To correct the first example, we must place a comma between the first (independent) clause and the second (dependent) clause. To correct the second example, we must remove the FANBOYS conjunction *and.*

Correct:	The manufacturing company has created an advisory board to oversee the implementation of the new safety **regulations, several of which** have already been put into effect.
Correct:	The manufacturing company has created an advisory board of outside **experts, many of whom** are nationally recognized in their fields.

It is also possible to correct this type of comma splice by using the construction *with some (many, most, few, others) of them + gerund*. While this construction may sound odd to you, it is perfectly acceptable. For example:

Incorrect:	Killer whales have a varied **diet, some groups specialize** in fish and other groups concentrate on seals.
Correct:	Killer whales have a varied **diet, with some groups specializing** in fish and other groups concentrating on seals.

Although this construction contains a gerund, it frequently appears in **correct** answers. In such cases, grammar is more important than style. Comma splices are absolutely grammatically incorrect, whereas gerunds merely have the *potential* to create fragments or awkwardness; there is nothing inherently wrong with them, and when they create neither of those things, they are perfectly acceptable – even on the SAT.

Comma and Semicolon Exercises

In the following sentences, identify and correct any comma or semicolon error that appears. Some of the sentences may not contain an error. (Answers p. 171, Official Guide question list p. 147)

1. In large doses, many common substances found in household items have devastating effects, however, many toxicologists insist that they are thoroughly innocuous in minuscule amounts.

2. César Chávez became an iconic figure as the leader of the Farm Workers' movement, but it was as a martyr who embodied the contrast between Mexico and the United States that he commanded the most attention.

3. Presented by the Public Theater, the production of *The Tempest* involves a cast of nearly 200 actors, many of whom have never appeared on stage before.

4. African-American life during the 1920s was documented in great detail by the writers and artists of the Harlem Renaissance, far less is known about it during the 1930s.

5. Universities have historically offered a wide variety of continuing education classes, many of them are now offered over the Internet as well as in traditional classrooms.

6. When the Mayan city of Palenque was first discovered, it was overwhelmed by the plant life of the rain forest, today it is a massive archaeological site that attracts thousands of tourists each year.

7. The geologic instability known as the Pacific Ring of Fire has produced numerous faults, these cause approximately 10,000 earthquakes annually.

8. Freeways and transit systems have facilitated movement throughout the San Francisco metropolitan area, with millions of people taking up residence in the suburbs.

9. The First World War began in August of 1914, it was directly caused by the assassination of Archduke Franz Ferdinand of Austria by Bosnian revolutionary Gavrilo Princeps.

10. Many design movements have political or philosophical beginnings or intentions, but the art deco style was invented for purely decorative purposes.

11. Over the past several years, the country's food prices have increased dramatically, and they are now at their highest rate in two decades.

12. The black-backed woodpecker lives almost exclusively in severely burned forests, it thrives on insects that are adapted to fire and can detect heat up to 30 miles away.

13. International sports competitions are symbolic showdowns that are more about winning than about universal friendship, however, they are a far more civilized alternative to actual warfare.

14. Culture has become a force that may accelerate human evolution, because people have no choice but to adapt to pressures and technologies of their own creation.

15. Found in the depths of all the world's oceans, the vampire squid lives in a twilight zone that that contains extremely low levels of dissolved oxygen, most other sea creatures cannot inhabit such regions.

16. The eyes of many predatory animals are designed to enhance depth perception; however, in other organisms they are designed to maximize the visual field.

17. Paris is known as a world capital of movie-making, moreover, the city itself has played a central role in films of every imaginable genre.

18. The bowhead whales is thought to be the longest-living mammal in the world, with some individual animals reaching up to 200 years of age.

19. Sugar and cavities go hand in hand, therefore, dentists recommend that the amount of sugar people consume be kept to a minimum.

20. The Mid-Autumn Festival, a popular harvest festival celebrated in Asia, dates back 3,000 years to China's Shang Dynasty, and is traditionally held on the fifteenth day of the eighth month.

21. Carl Bohm was one of the most prolific German pianists and composers during the nineteenth century, few people would, however, recognize his name today.

22. Gwendolyn Knight painted throughout her life but did not start seriously exhibiting her work until relatively late; her first retrospective occurred when she was nearly eighty years old.

23. Despite strains, fractures and tears, many athletes continue to work out, consequently, at least one expert would say that they are addicted to exercise.

24. Frederick Law Olmsted, who designed New York's Central Park, also designed Montreal's Mount Royal Park, most of it is heavily wooded.

25. During the nineteenth century, Detroit's road transportation and railways system were improved, nevertheless, the city's manufacturing sector remained weak until after the Industrial Revolution.

20. GERUNDS AND WORDINESS

To reiterate: the correct answer in Fixing Sentences will always be the most concise grammatically correct option. This cannot be stated strongly enough.

Very often, conjunctions such as *so, because* and *in order to* will be unnecessarily re-written in an excessively wordy and awkward manner. Other times, extra words will simply be added onto an otherwise straightforward sentence.

Wordy: Every year, hundreds of wild stallions are hunted down by modern cowboys in the southwestern United States, **with the reducing of the horse population to more sustainable levels being their goal**.

Concise: Every year, hundreds of wild horses are hunted down by modern cowboys in the southwestern United States **(in order) to reduce** the population to more sustainable levels.

Unnecessarily wordy versions of sentences, as in the above case, will often be signaled by an excessive use of gerunds. Note that the first version of the sentence contains two gerunds while the second version contains none.

Below are some common SAT Fixing Sentences phrases in both their wordy and concise versions:

Wordy	**Concise**
Being that	Because
Because of (her/him) being	Because she/he was
Despite (her/him) being In spite of (her/him) being	Although she/he was
For the purpose of going	To go In order to go

Whenever possible, replace a gerund with a noun or pronoun + conjugated verb.

Incorrect: The renowned physicist's book has been praised **because of making** difficult concepts accessible to an audience with little mathematical knowledge.

Correct: The renowned physicist's book has been praised **because it makes** difficult concepts accessible to an audience with little mathematical knowledge.

So when is it ok to use a gerund...?

When standard usage requires one

Incorrect: The Spanish city of Cádiz held the distinction **to be** the only city in continental Europe to survive a siege by Napoleon.

Correct: The Spanish city of Cádiz held the distinction **of being** the only city in continental Europe to survive a siege by Napoleon.

To preserve parallel structure

Incorrect: The panelists at the conference are responsible both for presenting original research and **they respond** to questions about its potential applications.

Correct: The panelists at the conference are responsible both for presenting original research and **for responding** to questions about its potential applications.

To indicate method or means

No Gerund: Flaubert attempted to achieve stylistic perfection in his novels, **and he rewrote** each sentence ten times.

Gerund: Flaubert attempted to achieve stylistic perfection in his novels **by rewriting** each sentence ten times.

Gerunds vs. Present Participles

Present participles end in "–ing" (e.g. *going, playing, making*) and are identical in appearance to gerunds; however, the two forms have different functions. **While gerunds are verbs that act as nouns, participles are verbs that act as adjectives.** Participles can be used to modify nouns, pronouns (rare), and clauses.

It is important that you be able to recognize when an "-ing" word is acting as a participle vs. a gerund because unlike gerunds, present participles do **not** usually affect whether a particular Fixing Sentences answer is right or wrong.

On the SAT, present participles are typically used in two ways:

1) Immediately before a noun

2) To begin a participial phrase

Immediately before a noun

Participle: Although it lacks traditional circus elements such as animals and clowns, Cirque du Soleil is regarded by both audiences and critics as an **exciting** spectacle.

In the above sentence, the participle "exciting" simply modifies "spectacle." It does nothing to make the sentence unnecessarily wordy. Compare the version with the participle to the more awkward gerund version:

Gerund: **In spite of its lacking** traditional circus elements such as animals and clowns, Cirque du Soleil is regarded by both audience and critics as an exciting spectacle.

To begin a participial phrase

Participial phrases can appear in the beginning, middle, or end of a sentence. In Fixing Sentences, they appear primarily at the beginning (as introductory clauses describing the subject), although they do sometimes appear at the end as well.

Introductory Clause

Correct: **Rejecting** a quiet life in Norway, Roald Amundsen chose to seek his fortune at sea and became the first person to reach both the North and South Poles.

At the end of a sentence, a participial phrase is often used to replace a pronoun that lacks an antecedent, or to replace a passive and awkward construction. In Fixing Sentences, this usage is virtually always correct.

Missing Antecedent or Comma Splice

Incorrect: Artists are not frequently associated with domestic serenity, **which** makes literary families cells of both inspiration and psychological investigation.

Incorrect: Artists are not frequently associated with domestic serenity, **this** makes literary families cells of both inspiration and psychological investigation.

Correct: Artists are not frequently associated with domestic serenity, **making** literary families cells of both inspiration and psychological investigation.

Passive Construction

Incorrect: The notion that Shakespeare did not revise his works is logical, **and an explanation is therefore provided** for his ability to direct, write, and perform in multiple plays each year.

Correct: The notion that Shakespeare did not revise his works is logical, **providing** an explanation for his ability to direct, write, and perform in multiple plays each year.

In this case, you might ask why it isn't possible to just eliminate the *-ing* word entirely?

Shorter: The notion that Shakespeare did not revise his works is logical **because it provides** an explanation for his ability to direct, write, and perform in multiple plays each year.

Well, sometimes you won't have that option. The participle will be the best answer available because all of the other options will contain a serious error such as a missing verb, extreme awkwardness, or a comma splice.

To sum up: Although it may seem as if there are a lot of exceptions to the "no *-ing*" rule, these exceptions are rare. The bottom line is that if you stick to the clearest and most concise version of a given sentence, you'll probably be fine.

Gerund and Wordiness Exercises

Rewrite the following sentences to eliminate wordiness and incorrectly used gerunds. Some of the sentences may not contain an error. (Answers p. 172, Official Guide question list p. 148)

1. It can hardly be considered a surprise that Incan emperors covered themselves in gold because of holding themselves to be the sun's human incarnation.

2. The museum's artistic director has arranged the exhibition thematically, with the purpose being to provide a new understanding of the multifaceted complexity of Native American life.

3. In the early 1920's, the music industry was already well on its way to becoming a major business, producing millions of dollars worth of goods and exerting a strong influence on popular culture.

4. Despite the fact of being a smaller city than either London or New York, Dublin possesses a thriving theater scene whose productions regularly achieve international renown.

5. Heralds were the predecessors of modern diplomats, traveling under the orders of kings or noblemen in order to convey messages or proclamations.

6. Bongoyo Island, located off the coast of Tanzania, has become a popular vacation spot for both tourists and Tanzanians because of it having such close proximity to the mainland.

7. The Province House, home to royal governors in seventeenth-century Massachusetts, was considered one of the grandest examples of colonial architecture because of possessing beautiful Tudor-style chimneystacks.

8. Contrary to popular belief, people should alternate rooms while studying because of retaining more information that way.

9. Some excellent teachers prance in front of the classroom like Shakespearean actors, while others are notable because of their being aloof or timid.

10. Having trained as a dancer for much of her life, Mae Jemison rejected a career in ballet in order to study engineering and in 1987 became a member of NASA's astronaut-training program.

11. *Prince Jellyfish*, an unpublished novel by author and journalist Hunter S. Thompson, was rejected by a number of literary agents because of lacking popular appeal.

12. Large sections of the Great Lakes often freeze in winter, thereby forcing manufacturers to find other methods of shipping their goods.

13. In spite of traffic often blocking its main arteries, East London contains side streets that can, on occasion, be as tranquil and pleasant as country lanes.

14. In scientific fields, scale models known as homunculi are often used for the purpose of illustrating physiological characteristics of the human body.

21. PASSIVE VOICE

In an **active** construction, the subject of a sentence typically precedes the object:

William Shakespeare	wrote	*Hamlet.*
Subject	**verb**	**object**

In a **passive** construction, on the other hand, the subject and the object are flipped. The passive voice also includes a form of the verb *to be* + past participle and the preposition *by*.

Hamlet	was written	by	William Shakespeare.
subject	**verb**	**prep**	**object**

Because passive constructions are always wordier than active ones, answers that include them are generally incorrect.

Active	**Passive**
Elena **drinks** the water.	The water **is drunk by** Elena.
The students in Professor Garcia's Chemistry class **conducted** an experiment yesterday.	An experiment **was conducted by** the students in Professor Garcia's Chemistry class yesterday.
A lack of concern for workers' environments **causes** some tensions between bosses and their employees.	Some tensions between bosses and their employees **are caused by** a lack of concern for workers' environments.

Passive Required

You will, however, sometimes have to choose a passive option in order to correct a more serious error such as a dangling modifier.

Incorrect: With its steep hills and stunning views of the surrounding harbor, visitors to San Francisco are unlikely to forget it.

Correct: With its steep hills and stunning views of the surrounding harbor, San Francisco **is** unlikely to be forgotten **by** visitors.

In addition, SAT will occasionally test this rule in reverse: a verb that requires the passive voice will be made active. In such cases, you must choose the passive option in order for the sentence to make sense.

Incorrect: The musician **admired** by his fans for his ability to make instruments out of everyday objects.

Correct: The musician **is admired** by his fans for his ability to make instruments out of everyday objects.

Passive Voice Exercises

In the following sentences, rewrite passive constructions to make them active. Some sentences may require the passive voice. (Answers p. 173, Official Guide question list p. 149)

1. In the later works of Nikola Stoyanov, also known by the pseudonym Emiliyan Stanev, nature is often described in great detail by the author.

2. Michael J. Rosen has written works ranging from picture books to poetry, and several anthologies varying almost as broadly in content have also been edited by him.

3. In the movie *The Killing Fields*, Cambodian photojournalist Dith Pran was portrayed by first-time actor Haing S. Ngor, a role for which Ngor won an Academy Award.

4. Although desserts typically characterized by their sweetness, bakers are now creating ones that feature intriguing blends of sweet and savory.

5. *The Nereus*, a remotely operated underwater hybrid vehicle, was designed by scientists at the Woods Hole Oceanographic Institute to function at depths of up to 36,000 feet.

6. Michael Balls, a British zoologist and biology professor, is known by many pharmaceutical company executives as an outspoken opponent of animal laboratory testing.

7. Between the late 1970s and 1980s, nine albums were recorded by Jamaican reggae musician Lone Ranger, born Anthony Alphonso Waldron.

8. Time Lapse Dance, a New York-based dance company whose mission is to provide modern reinterpretations of classic works, was founded by performance artist Jody Sperling in 2000.

9. Murtabak, a dish composed of mutton, garlic, egg, onion, and curry sauce, is frequently eaten by people throughout the Middle East, Singapore, and Indonesia.

10. Over the last thirty years, many forms of meditation have been examined by researchers, and a number of them have been deemed ineffective.

22. MODIFICATION ERRORS

In any given sentence, modifiers should be placed as close as possible to the nouns, pronouns, or phrases they modify; sentences that separate modifiers from the things they modify are often unclear and sometimes completely absurd.

Two kinds of modification errors are tested on the SAT:

1) Dangling Modifiers

2) Misplaced Modifiers

Dangling Modifiers

Dangling modifiers are one of the most frequent errors that appear exclusively in Fixing Sentences. Virtually every section will have at least one and as many as four questions that test your knowledge of them. It is therefore important that you be able to recognize this error quickly and easily.

Sentences that include dangling modifiers are characterized by an introductory clause that describes the subject but does not name it. This clause is always set off from the rest of the sentence by a comma.

Whenever a sentence contains such an introductory clause, the subject must appear immediately after the comma. If the subject does not appear there, the modifier is said to be dangling, and the sentence is incorrect.

> Incorrect: An elementary school teacher from Arkansas, increased funding and support for public libraries were what Bessie Boehm Moore advocated for.

The first thing we can note about the above sentence is that it contains an introductory clause (*An elementary school teacher from Arkansas*) that does not name the subject – it does not tell us who the elementary school teacher from Arkansas *is*.

We must therefore ask ourselves whom or what it is referring to. When we look at the rest of the sentence, it is clear that this description can only refer to Bessie Boehm Moore.

The words *Bessie Boehm Moore* do not appear immediately after the comma, so the modifier is dangling.

In order to fix the sentence, we must place Bessie Boehm Moore's name after the comma.

> Correct: An elementary school teacher from Arkansas, **Bessie Boehm Moore** advocated for increased funding and support for public libraries.

One very common SAT trick is to put a possessive version of the subject immediately after the introductory clause. In general, any possessive noun placed immediately after an introductory clause will be incorrect.

> Incorrect: An elementary school teacher from Arkansas, **Bessie Boehm Moore's goal** was to achieve increased funding and support for public libraries.

At first glance, this sentence looks and sounds correct. But who is the elementary school teacher from Arkansas? *Bessie Boehm Moore*, not her *goal*. And here, the *goal* is the subject – not *Bessie Boehm Moore*. The modifier is therefore dangling.

> Correct: An elementary school teacher from Arkansas, **Bessie Boehm Moore** had the goal of achieving increased funding and support for public libraries.

When fixing dangling modifiers, it is most important that you identify the subject – the rest of the sentence is not nearly as important – because when you look at the answer choices, you are looking for an option that places the subject immediately after the introductory clause. If the subject is not there, you can immediately eliminate the option.

The presence of a participle, particularly a present participle, at the beginning of a sentence often signals a dangling modifier.

In addition: it is acceptable to begin the main clause with an adjective or adjectives describing the subject because that description is considered part of the complete subject.

In the sentences below, the participles are in bold and the complete subject is underlined.

Present Participle

> Incorrect: **Stretching** from one end of the city to the other, the efficiency of <u>the new tram system</u> often surprises both tourists and city residents.

> Correct: **Stretching** from one end of the city to the other, <u>the new tram system</u> often surprises both tourists and city residents with its efficiency.

Past Participle

> Incorrect: **Born** in a small town in Missouri, the majority of <u>singer and actress Josephine Baker</u>'s career was spent performing throughout Europe.

> Correct: **Born** in a small town in Missouri, <u>singer and actress Josephine Baker</u> spent the majority of her career performing throughout Europe.

In general, dangling modifier answer choices follow a highly predictable pattern. Of five choices, only two will successfully place the subject after the introductory clause and correct the dangling modification; the other three can be eliminated immediately. Of the two that remain, one will be wordy and awkward, and the other will be correct. While it is always a good idea to read both answers, the shorter one will usually be right.

Occasionally, however, you will have no choice but to rearrange the entire sentence. For example:

> Correct: The train system stretches from one end of the city to the other and often surprises tourists and city residents with its efficiency.

> Correct: The train system, which stretches from one end of the city to the other, often surprises tourists and city residents with its efficiency.

Dangling Modifier Exercises

In the following exercises, identify the subject of each sentence, and rewrite as necessary to eliminate any dangling modifier that appears. Some of the sentences may not contain an error. (Answers p. 173, Official Guide question list p. 149)

1. Characterized by scenes that are shot quickly and in real time, low budgets and simple props are both typical elements of guerilla filmmaking.

2. Located in the southern Andes and covered by glaciers, the most recent eruption of the volcano known as Tronador occurred many centuries ago.

3. Born in St. Lucia in the West Indies, author Derek Walcott's work includes a number of plays and poems, most notably *Omeros*.

4. One of hundreds of islands that form the Indonesian archipelago, the width of Bali is less than 100 miles, yet it holds within its borders a rich and dramatic history.

5. Historically based on the carving of walrus ivory, which was once found in abundance, since the mid-twentieth century Inuit art has also included prints and figures made from soft stone.

6. One of the greatest musicians of her time, Clara Wieck's piano studies began when she was five years old; by the age of twelve she was renowned as both a performer and a composer.

7. Raised in Hong Kong and Shanghai before he moved to the United States in 1935, the buildings designed by I.M Pei are immediately recognizable because of their characteristic glass exteriors and use of geometrical forms.

8. Projecting an image of pain and brutality that has few parallels among advanced paintings of the twentieth century, *Guernica* was painted by Pablo Picasso in the aftermath of a World War II bombing.

9. Though educated and well mannered, the status of Jane Eyre remains low throughout the majority of the novel that bears her name.

10. Born at Dromoland Castle in County Clare, Ireland in 1821, artist and engineer George O'Brien's aristocratic background seemed at odds with his life in the Australian outback.

11. A member of the ruralism movement, Czech writer Josef Holocek made life in Bohemia one of the principal subjects of his work.

12. Despite winning several architectural awards, the impractical layout of the university's new dormitory has been criticized by students.

13. One of the earliest authorities to take a stand against pollution, it was proclaimed by King Edward I in 1306 that sea coal could not be burned because the smoke it created was hazardous to people's health.

14. Predicting renewed interest in their country's natural resources, a plan has been established by political leaders to create mines in the most underdeveloped regions.

15. Having remained under Moorish rule until the twelfth century, Arabic was still spoken by many Spaniards when their cities first came under the control of European monarchs.

Misplaced Modifiers

Although misplaced modifiers are far less common than dangling modifiers, they do appear from time to time. They may also, in very rare instances, appear in the Error-Identification section.

Unlike dangling modifiers, misplaced modifiers do not necessarily involve introductory clauses and can occur anywhere in a sentence. They do, however, also involve modifiers separated from the words or phrases they are intended to modify and often result in sentences whose meanings are unintentionally ridiculous.

Incorrect: Paul Conrad was a cartoonist known for his political satires that spent nearly three decades on staff at *The Los Angeles Times*.

Even though it's pretty obvious what the sentence is *trying* to say (logically, a satire cannot work at a newspaper), you need to pay close attention to what the sentence is *actually* saying. And what the above sentence is saying is that the **political satires** spent three decades on staff at *The Los Angeles Times*, when it was clearly **Conrad** who spent three decades working at that newspaper.

In order to correct the sentence, we need to make it clear Conrad, not the political satires, worked at the newspaper. There are a number of ways to make this correct, and there is no one structure that the SAT prefers. Below are a variety of structures that correct the misplaced modification in the original sentence.

Correct: Paul Conrad, a cartoonist known for his political satires, spent nearly three decades on staff at *The Los Angeles Times*.

Correct: Paul Conrad, who spent nearly three decades on staff at *The Los Angeles Times*, was a cartoonist known for his political satires,

Correct: Paul Conrad was a cartoonist known for his political satires; he spent nearly three decades on staff at *The Los Angeles Times*.

Correct: Known for his political satires, Paul Conrad spent nearly three decades on staff at *The Los Angeles Times*.

Misplaced Modifier Exercises

In the following sentences, correct any misplaced modification error that occurs. Some of the sentences may not contain an error. (Answers p. 174, Official Guide question list p. 149)

1. The Spanish city of Valencia is the birthplace of horchata, a drink said to date from the eighth century made from the juice of tiger nuts.

2. Claude McKay was one of the most important poets of the Harlem Renaissance that moved to New York after studying agronomy in Kansas.

3. The California Street Cable Railroad is an established public transit company in San Francisco, which was founded by Leland Stanford.

4. Many police officers have switched from patrolling city streets on horseback to patrolling them in cars, which have become the most popular form of urban transportation.

5. Praised by consumer magazines for being both versatile and affordable, the food processor performs a wide range of functions, including chopping, dicing, and pureeing, when flipping a switch.

6. Many ancient cities were protected from bands of invaders by fortresses roaming in search of settlements to plunder.

7. Some of the world's fastest trains run between the cities of Tokyo and Kyoto, which can reach speeds of up to 200 miles per hour.

8. Originally constructed during the Roman Republic, the House of Livia contains brightly colored frescoes dating back to the first decades B.C. that depict bucolic landscapes and mythological scenes.

9. The Georgian port of Batumi fell into decline in the mid-twentieth century, which once housed some of the world's first oil pipelines.

10. The bass viol has experienced a resurgence in popularity over the past several decades resembling the cello.

23. PARALLEL STRUCTURE II: PHRASES

Unlike the "list" form of parallel structure described in Chapter Seven, this kind of parallel structure requires you to work with phrases rather than single words. And also unlike list parallel structure, it usually – though not always – involves only two items.

The most difficult "phrase" parallel structure questions typically appear at the end of Fixing Sentences – usually as one of the last three questions, most often as the final question. In their simpler form (see the first example below), they may also occasionally appear in the Error-Identification Section or at the beginning of Fixing Sentences.

Since you will most likely encounter these questions after sitting through more than four hours of test-taking, the point at which you are most likely to be fatigued, it is important that you be able to recognize them without too much effort. These questions can be identified by the presence of certain conjunctions or comparisons:

-And
-But
-Not only…but also
-So…that
-At once…and
-Both…and
-Any other word pair (for the complete list, see p. 54-55)

If one of these conjunctions appears on the final sentence of a Fixing Sentences section, it is virtually guaranteed to be a parallel structure question. The rule is as follows:

The construction on one side of any given conjunction or comparison must match the construction on the other side of the conjunction or comparison as closely as possible.

If one side contains the construction *noun + preposition + noun*, the other must contain *noun + preposition + noun*; if one side contains a preposition, the other must contain a preposition, etc.

If the two sides do not match in their constructions, the result is an error in parallel structure.

Let us consider the following sentence:

Incorrect: More than simply providing badly needed space in cramped cities, skyscrapers **connect** people, <u>and</u> **creativity is fostered** in them.

The presence of the word *and* tells us that the constructions on either side of it must match. But since one side is active and the other passive, the construction is not parallel. To correct it, we must make both sides active:

Correct: More than simply providing badly needed space in cramped cities, skyscrapers **connect** people <u>and</u> **foster** creativity.

Now we're going to try something a little harder:

Incorrect: The researchers called for enforcement of existing cigarette sale regulations as well as investigating teenagers' motivations for smoking.

In the above sentence, the construction on either side of the conjunction *as well as* must be the same. So next we want to look at the specific construction of those two pieces of information. What did the researchers call for?

1) **enforcement** of existing cigarette sale regulations

2) **investigating** teenagers' motivations for smoking

When we examine the two sides, we see that their constructions do not match.

-The first one contains the classic *noun + of + noun* structure (*enforcement of… regulations*).

-The second contains a *gerund + noun* structure (*investigating…motivations*).

To make the two sides parallel, we must replace the gerund *investigating* with its noun form, *investigation*, and add *of*.

Correct: The researchers called for **enforcement <u>of</u> existing cigarette sale regulations** <u>as well</u> <u>as</u> **an investigation <u>of</u> teenagers' motivations for smoking**.

Occasionally, this type of parallel structure question will include a third item.

Incorrect: A remarkable self-publicist, Margaret Cavendish was a composer <u>of</u> poetry, a writer <u>of</u> philosophy, **plus she invented romances**.

Correct: A remarkable self-publicist, Margaret Cavendish was a composer <u>of</u> poetry, a writer <u>of</u> philosophy, and **an inventor <u>of</u> romances**.

Important: parallel structure questions frequently double as word-pair questions. If you can spot the word pair, you can often eliminate several answers immediately. For an example, see p. 130.

Parallel Structure with Adjectives

Although questions testing parallel structure with adjectives are extremely rare, they do occur, and they differ from other types of parallel structure questions in one important way: two adjectives can be paired with a single verb, making it **unnecessary** to repeat the verb for the second item. This construction falls into the category of "sounds wrong but is perfectly acceptable." For example:

Correct: After waiting more than an hour for the candidate to make his scheduled appearance, the voters **grew** <u>impatient</u> and the reporters <u>irritated</u>.

In the above sentence, the verb *grew* "applies" to the second adjective, *irritated*, as well as the first, *impatient*. Most people's inclination, however, would be to rewrite the sentence as follows:

Correct: After waiting more than an hour for the candidate to make his scheduled appearance, the voters **grew** <u>impatient</u> and the reporters **grew** <u>irritated</u>.

While this version of the sentence is correct, it is not inherently *more* correct than the first version, and you will never be asked to choose between the two. You will, however, be given only the first option as a correct answer and must recognize that it is acceptable.

Parallel Structure II: Phrase Exercises

In the following sentences, identify the conjunction or comparison indicating that parallel structure is required, and rewrite the sentence to include a parallel construction. Some of the sentences may not contain an error. (Answers p. 174, Official Guide question list p. 144)

1. Hans Holbein was one of the most exquisite draftsmen of all time, renowned for the precise rendering of his drawings and the compelling realism of his portraits.

2. The figure skater was praised not only for her mastery of difficult technical skills, but also her performance was elegant and graceful.

3. While the novel has many detractors, it also has many admirers who argue that its popularity is based on its gripping storyline and its characters' motives are believable.

4. Known for her musical compositions as well as for her poems and letters, Hildegard of Bingen was just as renowned in the twelfth century as the twentieth.

5. The university is installing an electronic course-evaluation system so that students can decide whether they should register for certain classes or should they avoid them altogether.

6. For fans of the legendary food writer Charles H. Baker, the contents of a dish are less compelling than what the story is behind it.

7. During the sixteenth century, an outbreak of fighting in Europe led to the invention of new weapons and to old weapons growing and evolving.

8. In contemporary education, there is a disturbing contrast between the enormous popularity of certain approaches and the lack of credible evidence for their effectiveness.

9. The development of identity was one of psychologist Erik Erikson's greatest concerns, both in his own life and his theory.

10. The bass clarinet, although similar to the more common soprano clarinet, is distinguished both by the greater length of its body plus several additional keys are present.

11. At its peak, the Roman army was nearly unconquerable because of the discipline of its soldiers, the hard and effective training of its commanders, and its troops were exceptionally well-organized.

12. In the moments before the judges announced their decision, the contestants became visibly more anxious and the audience more enthusiastic.

24. THE SUBJUNCTIVE

The subjunctive is a verb form used to express necessity, requests, and suggestions. It is also used to talk about hypothetical situations – ones that have not actually happened by that could or might happen. The subjunctive is tested relatively infrequently, so you should focus on it only after you are comfortable recognizing more common errors.

Although I have chosen to discuss the subjunctive here, it is tested in Fixing Sentences as well as Error-Identification. **When a verb in the subjunctive is underlined in an Error-Identification sentence, it will generally be correct; only in Fixing Sentences will you be responsible for actually correcting errors that involve it.**

Present Subjunctive

The major distinction between **subjunctive** and **indicative** (regular) verbs occurs in the third person singular (*he*/*she*/*it*/*one*). While an *–s* is added in the indicative (e.g. *she goes*, *talks*, *works*), **no *–s* is added in the subjunctive**.

The easiest way to think of it is that present subjunctive = infinitive minus the word *to*. Thus, the subjunctive form of *to be* = *be*; the subjunctive form of *to have* = *have*; and the subjunctive form of *to do* = *do*. The present subjunctive can also be used to express hypothetical situation, as indicated by the word *should*.

<u>Indicative</u>	<u>Subjunctive</u>
The building **is** constructed.	The planning committee <u>requests</u> that the building **be** constructed
Sunita **finishes** her work.	The teacher <u>recommends</u> that Sunita **finish** her work.
If Cole **arrives** at six o'clock	**Should** Cole arrive at six o'clock If Cole **should** arrive at six o'clock

Past Subjunctive

The past subjunctive is used for hypothetical situations – ones that have not actually occurred. Clauses that include the past subjunctive thus often begin with *if*. In the past subjunctive, the verb *to be* is always conjugated as *were*, never *was*.

<u>Indicative</u>	<u>Subjunctive</u>
The building **was** constructed.	If the building **were** (to be) constructed **Were** the building constructed
Sunita **finished** her work early.	If Sunita **had finished** her work early **Had** Sunita **finished** her work early (NOT: If Sunita **would have finished** her work early)
Cole **arrived** home at six o'clock.	If Cole **were to have arrived** at six o'clock **Were** Cole **to have arrived** at six o'clock

Subjunctive Exercises

In the following sentences, identify whether the underlined verb form is correct as is or should be changed to a different form. (Answers p. 174)

1. Although the "Mona Lisa" was painted in Italy, the French government insists that it **remain** in Paris because it has been exhibited continuously at the Louvre since 1797 and is considered French property.

   Correct   **Incorrect**

2. It is necessary that the government **works** together with private industry in order to find a means of providing safe drinking water for those living in rural areas.

   Correct   **Incorrect**

3. **Were** his longevity claim confirmed, Carmelo Flores Laura, a former rancher from Bolivia, would have the longest verified lifespan of anyone in human history.

   Correct   **Incorrect**

4. **Should** the restoration of the sculpture garden be carried out as planned, the statues will appear much as they did in when they were first created in the seventeenth century.

   Correct   **Incorrect**

5. If the museum **were** to obtain Frieda Kahlo's iconic self-portrait to include in its exhibition of her work, thousands of visitors would most likely attend.

   Correct   **Incorrect**

6. **Had** the Albert Bridge been demolished, as some city planners urged, Tower Bridge would have become the only bridge in London to exist in its original form.

   Correct   **Incorrect**

7. If astrophysicists **would have succeeded** in demonstrating that the matter in a black hole is permanently destroyed when the hole explodes, a central tenet of Einstein's mass conversion principle would be disproven.

   Correct   **Incorrect**

8. The space shuttle's launch would have been delayed for at least another six weeks if the stormy weather **did not clear** in time for it to take off.

   Correct   **Incorrect**

9. If the current market trend **were to continue**, the majority of mobile phone manufacturers would go out of business rather than continue to lose money and customers to a small number of competitors.

   Correct   **Incorrect**

10. Although the oil company's lawyers have tried to suppress the report describing the impact of the oil spill on protected wetlands, journalists are demanding that it **be** made available to the public.

    Correct   **Incorrect**   Correction: _____

25. MISCELLANEOUS: FIXING SENTENCES

Errors with *because*

The SAT likes to test your knowledge of the word *because*, and there are several predictable ways in which it does so.

A noun cannot "be because"

An event can only *take place* or *occur*, it cannot *be because*.

Incorrect:	**The beginning** of the American Civil War **was because** of a skirmish that broke out at Fort Sumter in South Carolina.
Correct:	**The beginning** of the American Civil War **occurred** when a skirmish broke out at Fort Sumter in South Carolina.
Even Better:	**The American Civil War began** when a skirmish broke out at Fort Sumter in South Carolina.

Redundancy

- The reason is because
- Because…is the reason that
- Because…is why

All of these phrases are redundant and thus **incorrect**. Use either *the reason is that* or simply *because*.

Note: The SAT rarely tests *the reason is because* in isolation – it is usually accompanied by another problem such as an unnecessary gerund or extreme wordiness. Knowing *the reason is that* is the correct phrase can, however, help you spot the right answer more quickly when this error does appear.

Incorrect:	In the 1970's, Quito, the capital of Ecuador, was named a World Heritage Site, and **the reason is because** of its historic center being exceptionally well preserved.
Incorrect:	**Because** its historic center was exceptionally well preserved **is the reason that** Quito, the capital of Ecuador, was named a World Heritage Site in the 1970's.
Correct:	In the 1970's, Quito, the capital of Ecuador, was named a World Heritage Site **because** its historic center was exceptionally well preserved.

The question is whether, NOT the question is if

Incorrect: After the closing arguments of the trial, the members of the jury faced the
                question of **if** they should convict the defendant or, on the contrary, set him free.

Correct: After the closing arguments of the trial, the members of the jury faced the question
                of **whether** they should convict the defendant or, on the contrary, set him free.

The rule is the same for words like *debate, challenge, decide, choose,* and *argue*:

Incorrect: After the closing arguments of the trial, the members of the jury argued about **if** they
                should convict the defendant or, on the contrary, set him free.

Correct: After the closing arguments of the trial, the members of the jury argued about **whether**
                they should convict the defendant or, on the contrary, set him free.

Whereby and Thereby

Whereby means "by which," and although it may sound awkward, its appearance does not necessarily
indicate an incorrect answer.

Correct: Desalination is a process **whereby** salt and other minerals are removed from water in
                order to produce a liquid that is suitable for human consumption.

Thereby is a synonym for "thus" and "therefore" and can be used interchangeably with those words. Like
whereby, it may seem awkward but does not by itself indicate an incorrect answer.

Correct: The Scientific Revolution was an era in which new ideas in astronomy, biology, and
                medicine transformed medieval and ancient views of nature, **thereby** laying the
                foundation for most modern discoveries.

For all

This is a fairly common "trick" phrase in Fixing Sentences. It means *despite*, and don't get fooled because
you think it sounds funny. It's correct.

Correct: **For all** his interest in abstract forms, Picasso remained devoted to painting the human figure for
                much of his career.

Plus

The word *plus*, especially when it is followed by a gerund, is virtually always wrong.

Incorrect: Jonas Salk, the creator of the first polio vaccine, was seen by many as a savior **plus**
                achieving rapid fame.

Correct: Jonas Salk, the creator of the first polio vaccine, was seen by many as a savior **and**
                achieved rapid fame.

26. FIXING SENTENCES STRATEGIES

So now that you know what to look for, let's consider some strategies for identifying answers in Fixing Sentences.

Example #1

The landscapes of the Caribbean islands are famous for their jewel-like <u>beauty, and some of their most amazing scenery lies hidden underwater</u>.

(A) beauty, and some of their most amazing scenery lies
(B) beauty, and some of its most amazing scenery lies
(C) beauty, but some of their most amazing scenery lying
(D) beauty, some of their most amazing scenery lies
(E) beauty; however, some of their most amazing scenery lies

Shortcut: spot the conjunction error

An underlined conjunction in Fixing Sentences frequently indicates that the conjunction itself is being tested. So let's look at the relationship between the clauses:

Clause 1:   The landscapes of the Caribbean islands are famous for their jewel-like beauty.

Clause 2:   Some of their most amazing scenery lies underwater.

-The two clauses contradict one another, so we need a contradictor such as *but*. That eliminates (A) and (B).

-(C) contains a gerund, and (D) contains a comma splice, so we can eliminate them as well.

-So that leaves us with **(E)**.

You could also figure out the answer this way:

-Start by eliminating (C) because it contains a gerund and (D) because it contains a comma splice.

-(B) contains the singular pronoun *its*, while (A) and (E) contains the plural pronoun *their*. What's the antecedent? *landscapes*, which is plural, so that eliminates (B).

-(E) contains a correctly-used semicolon. When an answer choice contains a correctly-used semicolon, that answer is usually right.

Example #2

Frequently dismissed as a buffoonish entertainer during his lifetime, <u>some now recognize jazz musician Cab Calloway as a creative genius</u>.

(A) some now recognize jazz musician Cab Calloway as a creative genius

(B) a creative genius is what some now recognize jazz musician Cab Calloway to be

(C) jazz musician Cab Calloway is now recognized by some as a creative genius

(D) jazz musician Cab Calloway now being recognized by some people as a creative genius

(E) jazz musician Cab Calloway's music is now recognized by some as the product of a creative genius

Shortcut: The first thing we can notice about this sentence is that it contains an introductory clause that describes but does not name the subject; we don't know *who* was frequently dismissed as a buffoonish entertainer during his lifetime. The presence of that introductory clause suggests that we're probably dealing with a dangling modifier, so the first thing we need to do is identify the subject.

So *who* was frequently dismissed as a buffoonish entertainer during his lifetime?

Jazz musician Cab Calloway. So the correct answer must start with those words.

-That eliminates (A) and (B).

-E contains the classic trick of making the subject possessive (*Cab Calloway's*), so that's out too.

-That leaves us with (C) and (D).

-(D) contains the gerund *being*, so the answer is **(C)**.

Example #3

In order to be an effective driver, one must have both an understanding of how to handle a vehicle <u>plus being willing to obey traffic laws strictly</u>.

(A) as well as being willing to obey
(B) and having a willingness in obeying
(C) with a willingness for obeying
(D) as well as being willing to obey
(E) and a willingness to obey

Shortcut: look for the word pair.

Since *both* must go with *and*, we can immediately eliminate choices (A), (C), and (D).

Choice (B) is long, contains a gerund, and is un-idiomatic (the correct phrase is "willingness **to** obey"), so that leaves us with **(E),** which is the answer.

Fixing Sentences Test

1. <u>Benjamin Franklin demonstrated his enthusiasm for inoculation against smallpox, he collaborated</u> on many studies that demonstrated the procedure's effectiveness.

   (A) smallpox, he collaborated
   (B) smallpox, and he collaborated
   (C) smallpox by collaborating
   (D) smallpox and collaborating
   (E) smallpox, he was collaborating

2. <u>Although once being found in abundance</u> on the North American continent, many species of Amazon parrot have now become nearly extinct.

   (A) Although once being found in abundance
   (B) Although they were once found in abundance
   (C) Despite their being found once in abundance
   (D) Once they were found in abundance
   (E) Even though it was once found in abundance

3. Because they did not want to miss a second of the comet's collision with Jupiter, the astronomers <u>have kept</u> their telescopes fixed on the sky until the consequences of the impact became clear.

   (A) have kept
   (B) having kept
   (C) keep
   (D) kept
   (E) keeping

4. Amelia Griffiths, one of the most prominent amateur scientists of the early <u>nineteenth century, and she was a beachcomber and phycologist who made</u> many important collections of algae specimens.

   (A) nineteenth century, and she was a beachcomber and phycologist who made
   (B) nineteenth century, being a beachcomber and phycologist making
   (C) nineteenth century, was a beachcomber and phycologist who made
   (D) nineteenth century, a beachcomber and phycologist who made
   (E) nineteenth century, she was a beachcomber and phycologist who had made

5. Although most people do not realize it, <u>skiing on fresh snow, skating on reflective ice, and hikes at high altitudes</u> can expose people to more harmful ultraviolet rays than a day at the beach.

   (A) skiing on fresh snow, skating on reflective ice, and hikes at high altitudes
   (B) skiing on fresh snow, to skate on reflective ice, and to hike at high altitudes
   (C) to ski on fresh snow, to skate on reflective ice, and hiking
   (D) skiing on fresh snow, skating on reflective ice, and hiking at high altitudes
   (E) skiing on fresh snow and skating on reflective ice, hiking at high altitudes

6. Despite <u>negotiations that were threatening to collapse,</u> the senators were able to salvage the bill that they had worked so long to prepare.

   (A) negotiations that were threatening to collapse
   (B) negotiations whose collapse was threatening
   (C) negotiations, threatening to collapse
   (D) negotiations, for which collapse was a threat
   (E) negotiations where collapse was threatened

7. <u>Most often associated with medieval Europe, Japanese society was based on feudalism</u> during the same period.

   (A) Most often associated with medieval Europe, Japanese society was based on feudalism
   (B) Most often associated with medieval Europe, feudalism formed the basis of Japanese society
   (C) Most often associated with medieval Europe, Japanese society based on feudalism
   (D) Its association with medieval Europe occurring most often, Japanese society was based on feudalism
   (E) Being most often associated with medieval Europe, feudalism had also been the basis for Japanese society

8. <u>The mineral azurite has an exceptionally deep blue hue, and for that reason they have tended to be</u> associated since antiquity with the color of winter skies.

   (A) The mineral azurite has an exceptionally deep blue hue, and for that reason they have tended to be
   (B) The mineral azurite has an exceptionally deep blue hue, and this is why it has tended to be
   (C) The mineral azurite has an exceptionally deep blue hue, it has tended to be
   (D) The mineral azurite has an exceptionally deep blue hue, so they have often been
   (E) The mineral azurite has an exceptionally deep blue hue; therefore, it has often been

9. Responding to pressure from business leaders and politicians alike, <u>the labor union has announced that they will begin</u> to hold discussions about the proposed contract early next week.

    (A) the labor union has announced that they will begin

    (B) the labor union have announced that they would begin

    (C) the labor union announcing that they would begin

    (D) the labor union having announced that it would begin

    (E) the labor union has announced that it will begin

10. Cajun cuisine is predominantly rustic, relying on locally available ingredients <u>and preparation of it is simple</u>.

    (A) and preparation of it is simple

    (B) plus preparation being simple

    (C) and simple preparation

    (D) and preparation as simple

    (E) with simplicity in its preparation

11. By inspecting the language of close relationships, <u>a deeper understanding of the relationships themselves can be gained</u>.

    (A) a deeper understanding of the relationships themselves can be gained

    (B) a deeper understanding of the relationships themselves would be gained

    (C) this is how we can gain a deeper understanding of the relationships themselves

    (D) we can gain a deeper understanding of the relationships themselves

    (E) we would have gained a deeper understanding of the relationships themselves

12. Every chess game contains millions of potential moves, <u>which makes it impossible to predict</u> a player's strategy more than a few minutes into the future.

    (A) which makes it impossible to predict

    (B) making it impossible to predict

    (C) making it impossible in predicting

    (D) so predicting is not possible

    (E) it is therefore impossible to predict

13. The roundscale spearfish and the white marlin are two <u>separate, if closely related, species</u>.

    (A) separate, if closely related, species

    (B) separate species, although being closely related

    (C) separate species, but also closely related

    (D) separate species, whereas they are related closely

    (E) separate species, although their relationship is a close one

14. Patrons of the restaurant find it at once impressive because of its superior <u>quality, but its poor service makes eating there unpleasant</u>.

    (A) quality, but its poor service makes eating there unpleasant

    (B) quality, although its poor service makes it unpleasant for them to eat there

    (C) quality, and its poor service makes eating there unpleasant also

    (D) quality while having poor service that makes eating there unpleasant

    (E) and unpleasant because of its poor service

Answers can be found on page 175.

27. FIXING PARAGRAPHS: HALF READING, HALF WRITING

The Fixing Paragraphs section always contains six questions, divided into two types:

1) Grammar and Style

2) Paragraph Organization

The order of the questions follows the order of the paragraph (usually about 13-15 sentences long), and grammar/style and paragraph organization questions are distributed randomly. Some sections are divided evenly between the two kinds of questions, while others include mostly one kind or the other. Unfortunately, there is no way to predict which way a particular test might skew.

The most important thing to understand about Fixing Paragraphs is that it tests both reading and writing skills simultaneously. In fact, it can be helpful to think of the section as Critical Reading lite because it tests many of the same skills tested on Critical Reading, albeit in vastly simplified form. Unlike questions in the other two multiple-choice Writing sections, many Fixing Paragraphs questions do not concern isolated sentences that can be considered individually but rather sentences, or portions of sentences, that must be considered in context of the paragraph or passage as a whole. An answer choice that does not contain any grammatical errors will therefore not be correct if it does not make sense within the larger scope of the paragraph or passage.

In order to answer questions correctly, you must therefore understand the topic and main point of the overall passage as well as each paragraph. You must be able to identify information that accurately supports a given point and move beyond understanding how clauses within a single sentence relate to one another to recognizing how separate sentences relate to one another in the context of a paragraph. As a result, Fixing Paragraphs questions have a somewhat heavier emphasis on transitions than do either Error-Identification or Fixing Sentences questions.

Strategies for Approaching Fixing Paragraphs

Because so much of Fixing Paragraphs is based on context, you should aim to get a *general* understanding of the passage before you look at the questions. Most passages are fairly straightforward, if somewhat clunky and awkwardly written, and you do not need to spend time poring over every single word; rather, your goal should merely be to glance through the passage and get the gist of the topic and the information that each of the paragraphs contain. If you pay a reasonable amount of attention to topic sentences, you can likely skim through the bodies of paragraphs fairly quickly.

You should, however, mark any spot that contains a glaring grammatical error or that clearly seems strange or illogical; questions involving those places will almost certainly appear, and if you can notice them – or better, fix them – yourself ahead of time, you can make the section go much more smoothly.

If you have difficulty with the comprehension- and passage organization-based questions, you are probably best off skipping them upfront and doing the more straightforward grammar questions first so that you don't risk losing relatively easy points unnecessarily. Then, if you have time, you can come back to the remaining questions, starting with the one that seems most manageable and working your way to the most challenging in order to avoid spending time on questions that you might not answer correctly at the expense of ones that you almost certainly will.

Grammar and Style

Grammar and style questions are further broken down into two main categories:

- **Sentence Revision** questions require you to identify the best revision of a sentence or portion of a sentence.

- **Combining Sentences** questions require you to identify the best way to combine two sentences into a single sentence.

The most important thing to remember about grammar and style questions is that the rules they test are identical to those tested in Fixing Sentences. This means that all of the same grammar and style rules apply. To reiterate:

1) Shorter = Better

2) Gerunds = Bad

3) Passive = Bad

4) Comma Splices = Bad

So if a sentence seems to fit the context of a paragraph but violates one of the above rules, look again. There's probably a better answer.

Paragraph Organization

Paragraph organization and rhetoric questions typically appear in the following forms:

- **Sentence Insertion** questions require you to identify which new sentence should be inserted at a specific point in the paragraph.

- **Sentence Order** questions require you to identify where in the paragraph an existing sentence would best belong.

- **Information Insertion** questions require you to identify specific words or information that would strengthen a sentence or paragraph.

- **Transition** questions require you to identify which transition should be placed at the beginning of a given sentence.

- **Rhetorical Strategy** questions require you to identify a particular rhetorical strategy (e.g. personification, anecdote, analogy) used in a portion of the paragraph.

- **Paragraph Division** questions require you to identify where a paragraph break would most logically be inserted in a passage.

Since it's really not possible to closely examine how to approach these kinds of questions without an actual passage, let's look at one:

When Merriwether Lewis and William Clark set out in 1803 to explore the lands west of the Mississippi River, they couldn't make the journey alone. (1) The wilderness was dense, and Native American attacks were common. (2) Luckily, when Lewis and Clark arrived in what is now North Dakota, they met Sacagawea. (3) A member of the Shoshone tribe, her marriage to a French trader named Charbonneau had made Sacagawea accustomed to interacting with settlers. (4) She would go down in history for leading Lewis and Clark thousands of miles, from present-day North Dakota all the way to the Pacific Ocean. (5)

Although Sacagawea is famous for being Lewis and Clark's guide, she didn't just give them directions. (6) She did much more than that. (7) She served as an interpreter between the explorers and the Shoshone people. (8) So that they could interact peacefully. (9) Also, since women did not accompany war parties, her being there showed Native Americans that the explorers did not have hostile intentions and prevented conflicts between the two groups – with only one exception. (10) However, for most of the nineteenth century, Sacagawea was forgotten. (11) That changed in 1902, when suffragist Eva Emery Dye published *The Conquest: The True Story of Lewis and Clark*. (12) Since then, Sacagawea has been honored with countless memorials and statues. (13) Almost as soon as the book appeared, Sacagawea was quickly claimed as a hero by women's rights groups, and many books and essays were written about her. (14) Her face has even appeared on her own specially issued dollar coin. (15)

Rhetorical Strategy

An important strategy used in the first paragraph is to:

(A) present a difficult problem and describe its successful resolution
(B) explain the cultural advantages of bilingualism for members of the Shoshone tribe
(C) provide an explicit critique of early American policy toward Native Americans
(D) convey a detailed impression of the wilderness west of the Mississippi River
(E) compare the kinds of travel common in nineteenth century America to the kinds of travel common today

Strategy:

Although they appear on the Writing sections, questions like these are fundamentally about reading. The main thing to remember is that you should go back to the passage and sum up the focus of the first paragraph for yourself.

What does the first paragraph discuss? Why Lewis and Clark needed a guide (dense wilderness, Native American attacks) and how they found an excellent one (Sacagawea). In other words, a problem and its solution.

So the answer must be (A).

Don't be fooled by the fact that (A) doesn't explicitly include people or places mentioned in the passage. Just like Critical Reading questions, these kinds of writing questions will ask you to translate concrete information into a more abstract form.

Sentence Revision:

Which of the following is the best version of the underlined portion of sentence 3 (reproduced below)?

A member of the Shoshone tribe, her marriage to a French trader named Charbonneau had made Sacagawea accustomed to interacting with settlers.

(A) Sacagawea had become accustomed to interacting with settlers because of her marriage to a French French trapper named Charbonneau.

(B) Sacagawea's familiarity with how to interact with settlers was because of her husband Charbonneau, a trapper.

(C) a trapper named Charbonneau, to whom Sacagawea was married, is why Sacagawea was accustomed to interacting with settlers.

(D) it was because of her marriage to a trapper named Charbonneau that Sacagawea was accustomed to interacting with settlers.

(E) her being married to a trapper named Charbonneau had led to her being accustomed to interacting with settlers.

Strategy:

Let's go back to our Fixing Sentences rules and examine the construction of the original sentence. We notice that it begins with an introductory clause that describes but does not name the subject:

A member of the Shoshone tribe,

That tells us right away that we're probably dealing with a dangling modifier.

-Who was a member of the Shoshone tribe? Sacagawea.

So we know that the first word after the introductory clause must be the word *Sacagawea*.

That is only true of (A), so it must be the answer.

Information Insertion:

Paragraph two would best be improved by the addition of:

(A) the inclusion of specific words translated by Sacagawea

(B) an example of the kind of directions Sacagawea gave Lewis and Clark

(C) the name of a woman who was known for leading a war party

(D) more information about how Sacagawea's first encounter with settlers

(E) a description of a confrontation between Lewis and Clark and hostile Native Americans.

Strategy:

When faced with a question like this, you have two choices: you can either plug in the answer choices one by one, or you can start by going back to the passage and figuring out what's missing. While the former might feel safer, the latter is far more effective.

When we read through paragraph two, we notice that it ends rather abruptly. The majority of the passage focuses on Sacagawea's success in helping Lewis and Clark navigate their relations with Native Americans, but at the end, a new idea is suddenly introduced: we are told that there was a conflict, but that conflict is never explained. The most effective way to improve the paragraph would therefore be to provide more details about the conflict.

So the answer is (E).

Combining Sentences

In context, which is the best way to combine sentences 6 and 7 (reproduced below?)

She served as an interpreter between the explorers and the Shoshone people. So that they could interact peacefully.

(A) She served as an interpreter between the explorers and the Shoshone people, they could interact peacefully that way.
(B) She served as an interpreter between the explorers and the Shoshone people, whereas she allowed them to interact peacefully.
(C) She served as an interpreter between the explorers and the Shoshone people and allowing them to interact peacefully.
(D) She served as an interpreter between the explorers and the Shoshone people, whereby their peaceful interaction was allowed.
(E) She served as an interpreter between the explorers and the Shoshone people, allowing them to interact peacefully.

Strategy:

We're going to treat this exactly like a Fixing Sentences question.

Choice (A) contains a comma splice and can therefore be eliminated immediately.

The transition *whereas* in choice B incorrectly indicates a contradiction between the two ideas.

Choice (C) contains verbs whose tenses are not parallel and can be eliminated as well.

Choice (D) contains a passive construction, so that's gone too.

Which leaves us with (E).

Sentence Order

Where is the best place for sentence 14?

(A) where it is now
(B) after sentence 10
(C) after sentence 11
(D) after sentence 12
(E) after sentence 15

Strategy:

Instead of plugging sentence 12 into each of the answer choices (and wasting a lot of time in the process), we're going to figure the answer out logically.

Sentence 14 describes what happened *almost as soon as the book was published*. What book? Well, the only book that is mentioned is Eva Emery Dye's book in sentence 11. And if we're talking about what happened right after the book's publication, then that information should appear right after sentence 11.

So the answer is (C).

Transitions

Which of the following would most appropriately be inserted at the beginning of sentence 6 (reproduced below)?

She did much more than that.

(A) However,
(B) Essentially,
(C) Meanwhile,
(D) In fact,
(E) On the other hand,

Strategy:

This question requires us to determine the relationship between this sentence and the previous sentence. To do so, we must examine them separately and see if they are talking about the same idea or different ideas.

Sentence 1: Although Sacagawea is famous for being Lewis and Clark's guide, she didn't just give them directions.

Sentence 2: She did much more than that.

Both sentences contain the same idea. That eliminates (A), (C), and (E) because they would be used to connect two contradicting thoughts.

So that leaves us with (B) and (D).

Now we look more closely at the relationship between the sentences: the second sentence is emphasizing the information presented in the first, which means that (D), *In fact*, works.

Choice (B), *Essentially*, would be used to clarify or simply an idea, which is not quite what's going on here.

So the answer is (D).

Paragraph Division

Where is the most logical place to begin a new paragraph?

(A) After sentence 9
(B) After sentence 10
(C) After sentence 12
(D) After sentence 13
(E) After sentence 14

Strategy:

This question requires us to determine where in the passage the idea shifts. When we look back at the second paragraph, we see that sentences 6 through 10 describe events that occurred in Sacagawea's time, while sentences 11 through 15 describe how Sacagawea was viewed in later times. The logical break therefore occurs after sentence 10, when we move from a discussion of Sacagawea's ability to mediate between Lewis and Clark and the Shoshone people to the statement that Sacagawea was forgotten for most of the nineteenth century.

So the answer is (B).

Appendix A

Note: The following lists are based on the questions in the Official SAT Study Guide, Second Edition[1] (© 2009 by The College Board). In general, I have attempted to categorize each question according the *primary* concept it tests, even though there may be secondary errors contained in the answer choices (e.g. a question designed primarily to test pronoun-antecedent usage is listed as a pronoun-antecedent question, despite the fact that several of the answer choices contain improperly used gerunds). Whenever possible, I have also listed the sub-category into which each question falls. For cases in which a question truly does test multiple concepts simultaneously, however, I have listed it in multiple categories. "No error" questions are indicated as such and are also listed according to the primary concepts they test. Errors discussed in the book but not listed below are based on questions from released College Board exams not included in the Official Guide.

Key:

s-nec-v = subject – non-essential clause – verb

s-pp-v = subject – prepositional phrase – verb

pp-v-s = prepositional phrase – verb – subject

NE = No error

Subject-Verb Agreement (p. 12)

Test: 1	Section: 6	Question: 20	(NE, the number)	p: 410
Test: 1	Section: 6	Question: 23	(s-nec-v, s-pp-v)	p: 410
Test: 1	Section: 6	Question: 24	(NE)	p: 410
Test: 1	Section: 6	Question: 28	(s-pp-v)	p: 410
Test: 1	Section: 10	Question: 1	(there is/are)	p: 429
Test: 1	Section: 10	Question: 13	(s-pp-v)	p: 431
Test: 2	Section: 6	Question: 20	(simple disagreement)	p: 472
Test: 2	Section: 6	Question: 22	(s-pp-v)	p: 472
Test: 2	Section: 6	Question: 25	(s-nec-v)	p. 472
Test: 3	Section: 6	Question: 15	(relative clause)	p: 533
Test: 3	Section: 6	Question: 19	(s-nec-v)	p: 534
Test: 3	Section: 6	Question: 23	(compound subject)	p: 534
Test: 4	Section: 7	Question: 6	(NE, s-nec-v)	p: 600
Test: 4	Section: 7	Question: 27	(pp-v-s)	p: 602
Test: 5	Section: 6	Question: 3	(s-pp-v)	p: 656
Test: 5	Section: 6	Question: 7	(compound subject)	p: 657
Test: 5	Section: 6	Question: 19	(s-pp-v)	p: 659
Test: 5	Section: 6	Question: 26	(the number of)	p: 660
Test: 6	Section: 6	Question: 1	(s-pp-v)	p: 718

---

[1] There are seven tests in the second edition that overlap with the tests in the first (2005) edition. Test #4 in the second edition corresponds to Test #2 in the first edition; Test #5 in the second edition corresponds to Test #3 in the first edition, and so on.

Verb Tense and Form (p. 20)

Pronoun-Antecedent (p. 29)

Pronoun Case (p. 40)

Test: 2	Section: 6	Question: 12	p: 471
Test: 4	Section: 7	Question: 21	p: 602
Test: 4	Section: 7	Question: 26	p: 602
Test: 6	Section: 6	Question: 27	p: 721
Test: 7	Section: 4	Question: 14	p: 776
Test: 8	Section: 4	Question: 24	p: 839
Test: 9	Section: 3	Question: 28	p: 896
Test: 10	Section: 3	Question: 22	p: 957

Adjectives vs. Adverbs (p. 43)

Test: 1	Section: 6	Question: 14		p: 409
Test: 1	Section: 6	Question: 17		p: 409
Test: 4	Section: 7	Question: 29		p: 602
Test: 5	Section: 10	Question: 23	(NE)	p: 659
Test: 6	Section: 6	Question: 22		p: 721
Test: 7	Section: 4	Question: 13		p: 776
Test: 7	Section: 4	Question: 16	(NE)	p: 776
Test: 8	Section: 4	Question: 12		p: 838
Test: 8	Section: 4	Question: 15		p: 838
Test: 8	Section: 4	Question: 28	(NE)	p: 839
Test: 10	Section: 3	Question: 15		p: 956

Prepositions and Idioms (p. 48)

Test: 2	Section: 6	Question: 10	(NE, for all = ok)	p: 470
Test: 2	Section: 6	Question: 23	(arrived in)	p: 472
Test: 2	Section: 6	Question: 26	(offers of)	p: 472
Test: 4	Section: 7	Question: 25	(preoccupation with)	p: 602
Test: 4	Section: 10	Question: 6	(assert that)	p: 615
Test: 5	Section: 10	Question: 23	(NE)	p: 659
Test: 6	Section: 6	Question: 5	(determine whether)	p: 718
Test: 6	Section: 6	Question: 17	(condition for)	p: 720
Test: 6	Section: 6	Question: 21	(threat to)	p: 721
Test: 6	Section: 6	Question: 23	(NE)	p: 721
Test: 7	Section: 4	Question: 26	(regarded as/as being)	p: 777
Test: 8	Section: 4	Question: 18	(prefer to)	p: 838
Test: 8	Section: 4	Question: 23	(protest against, or) no preposition)	p: 839
Test: 8	Section: 4	Question: 28	(NE)	p: 839
Test: 8	Section: 10	Question: 8	(adopted by)	p: 863
Test: 9	Section: 3	Question: 24	(far from)	p: 895
Test: 9	Section: 3	Question: 25	(inconsistent with)	p: 896
Test: 9	Section: 3	Question: 29	(NE, intolerable to)	p: 896
Test: 10	Section: 3	Question: 23	(idiom, something of = ok)	p: 957
Test: 10	Section: 3	Question: 25	(listen to)	p: 957
Test: 10	Section: 10	Question: 1	(to think of something as)	p: 986

Parallel Structure (p. 46 & p. 121)

Test: 1	Section: 6	Question: 9		p: 408
Test: 1	Section: 10	Question: 12	(list)	p: 431
Test: 1	Section: 10	Question: 14		p: 431
Test: 2	Section: 6	Question: 1		p: 469
Test: 2	Section: 6	Question: 11	(NE)	p: 470
Test: 2	Section: 6	Question: 21		p: 472
Test: 2	Section: 10	Question: 8		p: 492
Test: 2	Section: 10	Question: 9		p: 492
Test: 3	Section: 6	Question: 7	(list)	p: 532
Test: 3	Section: 6	Question: 11		p: 532
Test: 3	Section: 6	Question: 12	(list)	p: 533
Test: 3	Section: 10	Question: 14	(NE)	p: 555
Test: 4	Section: 7	Question: 1		p: 599
Test: 4	Section: 7	Question: 6		p: 600
Test: 4	Section: 7	Question: 9	(list)	p: 600
Test: 4	Section: 7	Question: 10		p: 600
Test: 4	Section: 7	Question: 11		p: 600
Test: 4	Section: 7	Question: 20		p: 602
Test: 4	Section: 10	Question: 3		p: 614
Test: 4	Section: 10	Question: 4		p: 614
Test: 4	Section: 10	Question: 7		p: 615
Test: 4	Section: 10	Question: 13		p: 616
Test: 5	Section: 6	Question: 13		p: 658
Test: 5	Section: 10	Question: 6		p: 677
Test: 5	Section: 10	Question: 13	(NE)	p: 678
Test: 5	Section: 10	Question: 14	(NE)	p: 678
Test: 6	Section: 6	Question: 2	(list)	p: 718
Test: 6	Section: 10	Question: 5		p: 739
Test: 7	Section: 4	Question: 6		p: 775
Test: 7	Section: 4	Question: 11		p: 775
Test: 7	Section: 4	Question: 15		p: 776
Test: 7	Section: 4	Question: 17	(NE)	p: 776
Test: 7	Section: 10	Question: 10		p: 802
Test: 7	Section: 10	Question: 11		p: 803
Test: 7	Section: 10	Question: 12		p: 803
Test: 8	Section: 4	Question: 6	(list)	p: 837
Test: 8	Section: 4	Question: 9		p: 837
Test: 8	Section: 10	Question: 4	(list)	p: 862
Test: 9	Section: 3	Question: 8		p: 893
Test: 9	Section: 3	Question: 22	(list)	p: 895
Test: 9	Section: 10	Question: 5	(list)	p: 924
Test: 9	Section: 10	Question: 13		p: 926
Test: 10	Section: 3	Question: 9		p: 955
Test: 10	Section: 10	Question: 12		p: 987
Test: 10	Section: 10	Question: 13		p: 988

Faulty Comparisons (p. 51)

Test: 1	Section: 6	Question: 21		p: 410
Test: 1	Section: 6	Question: 29		p: 410
Test: 2	Section: 10	Question: 11		p: 492
Test: 3	Section: 6	Question: 13		p: 533
Test: 3	Section: 6	Question: 25		p: 534
Test: 4	Section: 7	Question: 1		p: 599
Test: 4	Section: 7	Question: 3		p: 599
Test: 5	Section: 6	Question: 27		p: 660
Test: 6	Section: 6	Question: 14		p: 720
Test: 6	Section: 10	Question: 2		p: 738
Test: 7	Section: 4	Question: 28		p: 777
Test: 7	Section: 10	Question: 13		p: 802
Test: 9	Section: 3	Question: 6		p: 893
Test: 9	Section: 3	Question: 7	(NE)	p: 893
Test: 9	Section: 10	Question: 14		p: 926
Test: 10	Section: 10	Question: 4	(NE)	p: 986

Word Pairs (p. 54)

Test: 1	Section: 6	Question: 18	(neither...nor)	p: 409
Test: 1	Section: 10	Question: 6	(so...that)	p: 430
Test: 2	Section: 6	Question: 15	(neither...nor)	p: 471
Test: 3	Section: 6	Question: 19	(both…and)	p: 534
Test: 3	Section: 10	Question: 9	(either…or)	p: 554
Test: 4	Section: 7	Question: 14	(either…or)	p: 601
Test: 4	Section: 10	Question: 11	(so…that)	p: 616
Test: 5	Section: 10	Question: 4	(no sooner…than)	p: 676
Test: 6	Section: 6	Question: 12	(as…as)	p: 720
Test: 6	Section: 6	Question: 28	(neither…nor)	p: 721
Test: 6	Section: 10	Question: 13	(so…that)	p: 740
Test: 7	Section: 4	Question: 10	(just as…so)	p: 775
Test: 8	Section: 4	Question: 29	(between…and)	p: 839
Test: 10	Section: 3	Question: 18	(neither…nor)	p: 956
Test: 10	Section: 10	Question: 12	(as…as)	p: 987

Noun Agreement (p. 59)

Test: 1	Section: 6	Question: 12		p: 409
Test: 1	Section: 10	Question: 3		p: 429
Test: 2	Section: 6	Question: 17		p: 471
Test: 3	Section: 6	Question: 4		p: 531
Test: 3	Section: 6	Question: 18	(NE)	p: 534
Test: 7	Section: 4	Question: 12		p: 776
Test: 8	Section: 4	Question: 25		p: 839
Test: 10	Section: 3	Question: 19		p: 957
Test: 10	Section: 3	Question: 28		p: 957

Comparatives vs. Superlatives (p. 61)

Relative Pronouns (p. 63)

Double Negatives and Double Positives (p. 66)

Conjunctions/Logical Relationship (p. 68)

Redundancy (p. 74)

Fragments/Non-Essential Clause Errors (p. 92)

Commas and Semicolons (p. 98)

Unnecessary/Incorrect Use of Gerund (p. 110)

Test: 1	Section: 6	Question: 2		p: 407
Test: 1	Section: 10	Question: 11		p: 431
Test: 2	Section: 6	Question: 4		p: 469
Test: 2	Section: 10	Question: 3		p: 491
Test: 2	Section: 10	Question: 1		p: 492
Test: 2	Section: 10	Question: 1		p: 492
Test: 3	Section: 6	Question: 2		p: 531
Test: 3	Section: 6	Question: 1		p: 533
Test: 3	Section: 10	Question: 3		p: 553
Test: 3	Section: 10	Question: 4		p: 553
Test: 5	Section: 6	Question: 1		p: 656
Test: 5	Section: 6	Question: 2		p: 656
Test: 5	Section: 6	Question: 5		p: 657
Test: 5	Section: 6	Question: 6		p: 657
Test: 5	Section: 6	Question: 9		p: 657
Test: 5	Section: 6	Question: 12		p: 658
Test: 5	Section: 6	Question: 15		p: 658
Test: 5	Section: 10	Question: 10		p: 677
Test: 6	Section: 6	Question: 5		p: 718
Test: 6	Section: 10	Question: 3		p: 738
Test: 6	Section: 10	Question: 8		p: 739
Test: 6	Section: 10	Question: 9		p: 739
Test: 7	Section: 4	Question: 4		p: 774
Test: 7	Section: 4	Question: 5		p: 775
Test: 7	Section: 4	Question: 6		p: 740
Test: 7	Section: 4	Question: 20		p: 777
Test: 7	Section: 4	Question: 22		p: 777
Test: 7	Section: 10	Question: 2		p: 801
Test: 7	Section: 10	Question: 7	(NE)	p: 802
Test: 8	Section: 4	Question: 2		p: 836
Test: 8	Section: 4	Question: 3		p: 862
Test: 8	Section: 10	Question: 7		p: 863
Test: 8	Section: 10	Question: 7		p: 863
Test: 8	Section: 10	Question: 14		p: 864
Test: 9	Section: 3	Question: 3		p: 892
Test: 9	Section: 10	Question: 2	(NE)	p: 924
Test: 9	Section: 10	Question: 3		p: 924
Test: 9	Section: 10	Question: 12		p: 925
Test: 10	Section: 3	Question: 1		p: 954
Test: 10	Section: 3	Question: 3		p: 954
Test: 10	Section: 3	Question: 7		p: 955

Gerund or Present Participle Required (p. 111)

Test: 2	Section: 6	Question: 8	p: 470
Test: 2	Section: 10	Question: 4	p: 491
Test: 3	Section: 10	Question: 8	p: 554
Test: 4	Section: 7	Question: 4	p: 599
Test: 4	Section: 10	Question: 5	p: 615

Test: 5	Section: 10	Question: 7	p: 677
Test: 10	Section: 10	Question: 5	p: 987
Test: 10	Section: 10	Question: 11	p: 987

Dangling Modifiers (p. 116)

Test: 1	Section: 6	Question: 7	p: 408
Test: 1	Section: 6	Question: 10	p: 408
Test: 1	Section: 10	Question: 5	p: 430
Test: 1	Section: 10	Question: 8	p: 430
Test: 1	Section: 10	Question: 9	p: 430
Test: 2	Section: 6	Question: 3	p: 469
Test: 2	Section: 6	Question: 7	p: 470
Test: 2	Section: 6	Question: 9	p: 470
Test: 2	Section: 10	Question: 6	p: 492
Test: 2	Section: 10	Question: 13 (NE)	p: 493
Test: 3	Section: 6	Question: 8	p: 532
Test: 4	Section: 7	Question: 5	p: 599
Test: 4	Section: 7	Question: 8	p: 600
Test: 4	Section: 7	Question: 11	p: 600
Test: 4	Section: 10	Question: 10	p: 616
Test: 4	Section: 10	Question: 12	p: 616
Test: 5	Section: 10	Question: 12	p: 677
Test: 6	Section: 6	Question: 6	p: 719
Test: 6	Section: 6	Question: 10	p: 719
Test: 6	Section: 10	Question: 14	p: 740
Test: 7	Section: 4	Question: 3	p: 774
Test: 7	Section: 10	Question: 1	p: 801
Test: 9	Section: 3	Question: 1	p: 892
Test: 9	Section: 10	Question: 7	p: 925
Test: 9	Section: 10	Question: 10	p: 925
Test: 10	Section: 3	Question: 5	p: 955
Test: 10	Section: 3	Question: 11	p: 955
Test: 10	Section: 10	Question: 6	p: 987

Misplaced Modifiers (p. 119)

Test: 3	Section: 6	Question: 16	p: 533
Test: 3	Section: 6	Question: 21	p: 534
Test: 3	Section: 10	Question: 2	p: 553
Test: 5	Section: 10	Question: 3	p: 676
Test: 7	Section: 10	Question: 14	p: 803

Active vs. Passive Voice (p. 114)

Test: 2	Section: 10	Question: 14	p: 493
Test: 3	Section: 10	Question: 7	p: 554
Test: 3	Section: 10	Question: 8	p: 554
Test: 5	Section: 10	Question: 4	p: 676
Test: 5	Section: 10	Question: 13	p: 678
Test: 7	Section: 4	Question: 1	p: 774

Miscellaneous

Redundancy

Appendix B: Questions by Test

Test 1

Section: 6 (p. 407)

1. Comma splice; gerund required to indicate means
2. Gerund
3. Fragment
4. Verb consistency
5. Conjunction
6. NE; main concept tested = tense consistency
7. Pronoun-antecedent: missing antecedent (it)
8. NE; main concept tested = non-essential clause
9. Parallel Structure; word pair
10. Dangling Modifier
11. Non-essential clause
12. Noun Agreement
13. NE; concepts tested = tense; adjective vs. adverb
14. Adjective vs. adverb
15. Verb consistency
16. Gerund vs. infinitive
17. Adjective vs. adverb
18. Word pair (neither…nor)
19. Pronoun-antecedent: (passengers = their, not "his or her")
20. NE; main concept tested = subject-verb agreement: the number of
21. Faulty comparison
22. Preposition; gerund vs. infinitive
23. Subject-verb agreement: s-nec-v
24. NE; main concept tested = subject-verb agreement: compound subject
25. Gerund vs. infinitive
26. Pronoun-antecedent: collective noun = singular
27. NE; main concepts tested: idiomatic usage (all more than, long since)
28. Subject-verb agreement: s-pp-v; between you and me
29. Faulty comparison

Section: 10 (p. 429)

1. Subject-verb agreement: there is/are
2. Antecedent-pronoun: missing antecedent (it)
3. Noun agreement
4. Antecedent pronoun: ambiguous antecedent
5. Dangling modifier
6. Word pair (so…that)
7. Miscellaneous: a noun cannot "be because"
8. Dangling modifier

9. Gerund/fragment
10. NE; main concept tested = non-essential clause
11. Gerund: being that = bad, because = good
12. Parallel Structure
13. Subject-verb agreement: s-pp-v
14. Parallel Structure

Test 2

Section: 6 (p. 469)

1. Parallel Structure
2. Non-essential clause/fragment
3. Dangling modifier
4. Gerund/wordy
5. Comma splice
6. Non-essential clause; passive
7. Dangling modifier
8. NE; main concept tested = gerund (required for idiomatic phrasing)
9. Dangling modifier
10. NE; main concept tested = idiom (for all their = correct)
11. NE; main concept tested = parallel structure
12. Pronoun Case (I vs. me)
13. Verb consistency (present vs. simple past)
14. Verb consistency; gerund
15. Word pair (either…or)
16. Tense: present perfect vs. simple past
17. Noun agreement
18. Pronoun-antecedent: tax = singular vs. plural (tax = singular, it)
19. NE; concepts tested = tense: present perfect ("has shown" = ok), long been = ok
20. Subject-verb agreement (managers = plural, holds = singular)
21. Parallel structure
22. Subject-verb agreement: s-pp-v
23. Preposition: arrived in
24. NE; concepts tested = tense: past perfect, negation (hardly anyone)
25. Subject-verb agreement: s-nec-v
26. Preposition: offers of
27. NE; main concept tested = "what" as subject
28. Pronoun-Antecedent: ambiguous antecedent
29. NE; concepts tested = gerund vs. infinitive, "herself" used for emphasis, idiomatic structure: "complicated as they were"

1. Tense: would; gerund
2. Non-essential clause; gerund
3. Gerund
4. Comma splice; gerund required (idiom)
5. Miscellaneous: it took + infinitive
6. Dangling modifier
7. NE; main concept tested = tense: would vs. will
8. Parallel structure
9. NE; concepts tested = parallel structure, word pair (both…and)
10. Conjunction; gerund (being that = bad, because = good)
11. Faulty comparison
12. Gerund; modification
13. NE; main concept tested = dangling modifier
14. Passive

Test 3

Section: 6 (p. 531)

1. Pronoun-antecedent (missing antecedent: it)
2. Gerund
3. NE; main concept tested = semicolon
4. Noun agreement
5. Non-essential clause
6. Verb consistency
7. Parallel structure
8. Dangling modifier
9. Non-essential clause
10. NE; main concept tested = pronoun-antecedent: collective noun = singular
11. Parallel structure
12. Parallel structure
13. Faulty comparison
14. Gerund/fragment
15. Subject-verb agreement
16. Misplaced modifier
17. Word pair (either…or)
18. NE; main concept tested = tense (present perfect, gerund vs. infinitive); noun agreement
19. Subject-verb agreement: s-nec-v
20. Pronoun-antecedent: singular/plural (other types = plural)
21. Misplaced modifier
22. Pronoun-antecedent: singular/plural (the gecko = singular)
23. Subject-verb agreement: compound subject = plural
24. Tense: present perfect vs. simple past
25. Faulty Comparison
26. Tense: past perfect (we had waited)
27. Pronoun-antecedent: collective noun = singular

28. NE; miscellaneous: although + adjective = ok
29. Redundancy

Section: 10 (p. 553)

1. NE; main concept tested = tense (would)
2. Misplaced modifier
3. Gerund/fragment
4. Verb consistency
5. Verb consistency
6. Comma splice, semicolon
7. Passive
8. Passive; present participle
9. Word pair (either…or)
10. Redundancy
11. NE; main concept tested = Semicolon
12. Non-essential clause
13. Miscellaneous: awkward phrasing
14. NE; concepts tested = comma splice, semicolon verb consistency, gerunds

Test 4

Section: 7 (599)

1. Faulty Comparison/parallel structure: missing preposition
2. Comma splice; pronoun-antecedent
3. Faulty comparison
4. Passive
5. Dangling modifier
6. Subject-verb agreement; "the reason is that"
7. NE; main concept tested = non-essential clause
8. Dangling modifier
9. Parallel structure
10. Verb consistency
11. Parallel structure
12. Verb consistency
13. Verb consistency
14. Word pair (either…or)
15. Pronoun-antecedent: singular vs. plural (shards = singular, its)
16. NE; subject-verb agreement: pp-v-s
17. NE; concepts tested = subject-verb agreement; tense (present perfect); adjective vs. adverb
18. Verb consistency
19. NE; main concept tested = relative pronoun (in which = ok)
20. Parallel structure
21. Pronoun case
22. Verb consistency; gerund vs. infinitive
23. NE; concepts tested = preposition, gerund vs. infinitive
24. Conjunction: double conjunction

25. Preposition: preoccupation with
26. Pronoun case (I vs. me)
27. Subject-verb agreement: pp-v-s
28. Pronoun-antecedent: singular vs. plural (tablets = plural, their)
29. Adjective vs. adverb

Section: 10 (p. 614)

1. Gerund vs. infinitive
2. Non-essential clause
3. NE; main concept tested = parallel structure
4. Parallel structure
5. Gerund required to indicate means
6. Preposition: "asserted" does not require a preposition
7. Parallel structure
8. NE; main concept tested = non-essential clause
9. Pronoun-antecedent: missing antecedent (this)
10. Dangling modifier
11. Word pair (so…that)
12. Dangling modifier
13. Parallel structure
14. Non-essential clause

Test 5

Section: 6 (p. 656)

1. Gerund
2. Gerund; no "would" in the same clause as "if" (choice E)
3. Subject-verb agreement: s-pp-v
4. Fragment
5. Non-essential clause; gerund; "do so" not "do it"
6. Pronoun-antecedent: missing antecedent (this)
7. NE; main concept tested = subject-verb agreement: compound subject
8. Gerund
9. Gerund
10. Comma + FANBOYS
11. Pronoun-antecedent: singular plural
12. Gerund/fragment
13. Parallel structure
14. Who vs. which
15. Tense; gerund
16. Gerund vs. infinitive
17. Conjunction
18. Double positive
19. Subject-verb agreement: s-pp-v
20. Pronoun-antecedent: singular vs. plural (crabs = plural, they)
21. Gerund vs. infinitive
22. Gerund vs. infinitive

23. NE; concepts tested = preposition, pronoun-antecedent, adjective vs. adverb
24. Comparative vs. superlative
25. Conjunction
26. Subject-verb agreement (the number of = singular)
27. Faulty comparison
28. Pronoun-antecedent: singular vs. plural (trucks = plural, they)
29. NE; main concept tested = comparative vs. superlative

Section: 10 (p. 676)

1. Tense: verb in simple past tense ("believed") requires "would," not "would have"
2. Non-essential clause
3. Misplaced modifier
4. Word pair (no sooner…than)
5. The reason that
6. Parallel structure
7. Gerund required to indicate means
8. NE; main concept tested = pronoun-antecedent, "which" used correctly to modify "programs"
9. Non-essential clause; gerund
10. Gerund; pronoun-antecedent: singular vs. plural (walruses = plural, they)
11. NE; main concept tested = tense: present perfect, used correctly with "since"
12. Dangling modifier
13. NE; main concept tested = parallel structure
14. Parallel structure: active vs. passive

Test 6

Section: 6 (p. 718)

1. Subject-verb agreement (s-pp-v)
2. Parallel structure: active vs. passive
3. Verb consistency
4. Double positive
5. Preposition: "determine" does not require a preposition
6. Dangling modifier
7. Miscellaneous: that = ok as subject
8. Pronoun-antecedent: collective noun (school) = singular
9. NE; main concept tested = tense: past perfect
10. Dangling modifier
11. NE: shortest and clearest
12. Word pair (as…as)
13. NE; main concept tested = would vs. will
14. Faulty comparison
15. Pronoun-antecedent: singular vs. plural (that/those)

16. NE: main concept tested = antecedent-pronoun: each = singular, its
17. Preposition: a condition for
18. Verb consistency: gerund vs. infinitive
19. Verb form: past participle vs. simple past (swam vs. swum)
20. Pronoun-antecedent: collective noun (agency) = singular
21. Preposition: a threat to
22. Adjective vs. adverb
23. NE; concepts tested = tense (present perfect) and preposition
24. Subject-verb agreement (s-nec-v)
25. Conjunction
26. Subject-verb agreement
27. Pronoun case
28. Word pair (neither…nor)
29. Subject-verb agreement (pp-v-s)

Section: 10 (p. 738)

1. Miscellaneous: wordiness
2. Faulty comparison
3. Non-essential clause; gerund
4. Antecedent-Pronoun: *which* ok, modifies *Kaissa*
5. Parallel structure
6. NE: main concept tested = antecedent-pronoun ("there" lacks an antecedent in C, D, and E)
7. Antecedent-pronoun: we…our
8. Parallel structure
9. Gerund
10. Antecedent-pronoun: singular vs. plural (programs = plural, they)
11. Miscellaneous: wordiness
12. Comma splice; wordiness
13. Word pair; wordiness
14. Faulty comparison

Test 7

Section: 4 (p. 774)

1. Passive
2. Conjunction; wordiness
3. Dangling modifier
4. Non-essential clause
5. Gerund
6. Parallel structure
7. Gerund; relative pronoun ("when" modifies nineteenth century)
8. Fragment
9. Semicolon
10. NE; main concept tested = word pair (just as…so)
11. Parallel structure

12. Noun agreement
13. Adjective vs. adverb
14. Pronoun case
15. Parallel structure
16. NE; main concept tested = tense, present perfect
17. NE; main concept tested = parallel structure
18. Conjunction
19. Subject-verb agreement (pp-v-s)
20. Gerund; tense: verb in simple past ("discovered") requires conditional: "a pass that *would* soon become"
21. Tense: past perfect
22. Gerund; "plus"
23. Pronoun-antecedent: you vs. one
24. NE; main concept tested: subject-verb agreement: s-pp-v
25. Pronoun-antecedent: a student = he or she
26. Gerund vs. infinitive OR idiom: regarded as (being)
27. Subject-verb agreement: s-pp-v
28. Faulty comparison
29. NE: main concept tested = long since

Section: 10 (p. 801)

1. Dangling modifier
2. Gerund
3. Miscellaneous: wordiness
4. Semicolon; pronoun-antecedent
5. Pronoun-antecedent: collective noun (fire department) = singular
6. Miscellaneous: modification. One does not watch "of television."
7. Parallel structure
8. Conjunction; logical relationship
9. Non-essential clause
10. Verb consistency; parallel structure
11. Parallel structure
12. Parallel structure: active vs. passive
13. Faulty comparison
14. Misplaced modifier

Test 8

Section: 4 (p. 836)

1. Fragment
2. Gerund
3. Run-on sentence
4. Gerund required to indicate means
5. Pronoun-antecedent: singular vs. plural (every = singular, her)
6. Parallel structure
7. NE; main concept tested = pronoun-antecedent, it = ok because antecedent is a gerund (finding)
8. Subject-verb agreement (s-nec-v)

9. Parallel structure
10. NE; main concept tested = pronoun-antecedent, "which" modifies "serious interest in drama"
11. Pronoun Antecedent: collective noun (empire) = singular
12. Adjective vs. adverb
13. Tense: would vs. will ("will" should not appear with a verb in the past)
14. NE; main concepts tested =
15. Adjective vs. adverb
16. Tense: past conditional vs. past ("would" indicates a recurring action in the past; "would have" is hypothetical indicates an action that did not actually occur)
17. Relative pronoun: who vs. which
18. Idiom: prefer x to y, not x more than y
19. Pronoun-antecedent: people = they, not "your"
20. Subject-verb agreement: s-pp-v
21. Tense: would vs. will
22. NE: main concept tested: would vs. will ("would" = ok because the sentence contains a verb in the past tense)
23. Preposition: protest against or no preposition
24. Pronoun case: between + me
25. Noun agreement
26. Pronoun-antecedent: "do so" not "do it"
27. Subect-verb agreement: s-pp-v
28. NE; main concepts tested = preposition, adjective vs. adverb
29. Word pair (between…and)

Section: 10 (p. 862)

1. Verb consistency/gerund
2. Miscellaneous: no comma between subject and verb
3. Gerund
4. Parallel structure
5. NE: main concept tested: although = ok without subject and verb after it
6. Conjunction
7. Non-essential clause; gerund
8. Preposition: adopted by
9. Conjunction
10. Non-essential clause
11. Non-essential clause
12. Pronoun-antecedent; semicolon
13. NE; concepts tested = gerund, wordiness, tense, conjunction
14. gerund; semicolon

Test 9

Section: 3 (p. 892)

1. Pronoun-antecedent: missing antecedent (that)
2. Verb consistency
3. Gerund
4. Subject-verb agreement: s-pp-v
5. Miscellaneous: wordiness
6. Faulty comparison
7. NE; main concept tested = faulty comparison
8. Parallel structure: missing preposition
9. Redundancy
10. NE; concepts tested = gerund, comma splice
11. Comma splice
12. Verb form: past participle vs. simple past (had written)
13. Double positive
14. Subject-verb agreement: there is/are
15. Relative pronoun: who vs. which
16. NE: main concept tested = comparative vs. superlative (two things compared so "more" is correct)
17. NE: concepts tested = pronoun-antecedent, gerund vs. infinitive, preposition
18. Subject-verb agreement = there is/are
19. Pronoun-antecedent: singular vs. plural (signs = plural, these or them)
20. Verb consistency
21. Subject-verb agreement: compound subject ("itself" = trick answer)
22. Parallel structure
23. Subject-verb agreement: s-pp-v
24. Preposition/idiom: far from
25. Tense: for = present perfect
26. Preposition: inconsistent with
27. Comparative vs. superlative
28. Pronoun case: between + me
29. NE; concepts tested = preposition, past perfect, "long since"

Section: 10 (p. 924)

1. Conjunction/logical relationship
2. Gerund; idiom: stated that
3. Gerund
4. Miscellaneous: wordiness
5. Parallel structure
6. Comma splice
7. Tense: would vs. will (sentence contains a verb in past tense, so "would" is required)
8. Non-essential clause; conjunction/logical relationship
9. Pronoun-antecedent: someone = he or she
10. Dangling modifier
11. Pronoun-antecedent: ambiguous antecedent (she)

12. NE; concepts tested = gerund, conjunction
13. Parallel structure: active vs. passive
14. Faulty comparison

Test 10

Section: 3 (p. 954)

1. Gerund
2. Fragment
3. NE; main concept tested = gerund, dangling modifier
4. Pronoun-antecedent: missing antecedent (they)
5. Dangling modifier
6. Comma splice; wordiness
7. Gerund
8. Miscellaneous: wordiness
9. Parallel structure
10. Pronoun-antecedent: singular vs. plural (it/their)
11. Dangling modifier
12. Subject-verb agreement (s-nec-v, verb before subject)
13. Gerund vs. infinitive
14. NE; main concept tested = gerund ok as subject
15. Adjective vs. adverb
16. Subject-verb agreement: s-pp-v
17. Verb consistency
18. Word pair (neither…nor)
19. Noun agreement
20. Tense
21. Relative pronoun (in which vs. that)
22. Pronoun case

23. NE; concepts tested: idiom (something of), "alike"
24. Subject-verb agreement (s-nec-v)
25. Preposition (listen to)
26. Pronoun-antecedent: ambiguous antecedent (she)
27. NE; main concept tested = comparative vs. superlative
28. Noun agreement
29. NE; concepts tested = subject-verb agreement (s-pp-v, "which" = singular) comparative vs. superlative

Section: 10 (p. 986)

1. Miscellaneous/idiom: to think of something "as if," not "that"
2. NE; main concept tested = subject-verb agreement (s-pp-v)
3. Comma splice; semicolon
4. NE: main concept tested = Faulty comparison
5. Gerund required to indicate means
6. Dangling modifier
7. Subject-verb agreement (s-pp-v)
8. NE; main concept tested = pronoun-antecedent ("which" is correctly used to modify "cost")
9. Passive
10. Semicolon; verb consistency
11. Participle required; wordiness
12. NE; concepts tested = parallel structure, word pair (as…as)
13. Parallel structure: verb form
14. NE; concepts tested = subject-verb agreement: compound subject; pronoun-antecedent: singular vs. plural (paint = singular, its)

ANSWER KEY

Identifying Parts of Speech (p. 8)

1. A: Adjective, B: Noun, C: Verb, D: Verb,
E: Adverb

2. A: Conjunction, B: Adjective, C: Pronoun, D:
Adverb, E: Preposition

3. A: Noun, B: Verb, C: Adverb, D: Preposition, E:
Noun

4. A: Adverb, B: Conjunction, C: Pronoun, D: Verb
(Infinitive), E: Adjective

5. A: Adjective, B: Preposition, C: Verb, D: Verb
(Infinitive), E: Verb

6. A: Noun, B: Verb, C: Verb, D: Noun, E: Preposition

7. A: Adjective, B: Noun (Singular), C: Verb, D:
Pronoun, E: Verb

8. A: Adjective, B: Verb, C: Adverb, D: Preposition, E:
Verb

9. A: Verb, B: Pronoun, C: Pronoun, D: Preposition, E:
Noun

10. A: Noun, B: Preposition, C: Verb, D: Preposition,
E: Noun

11. A: Preposition, B: Verb, C: Adjective, D: Verb, E:
Verb

12. A: Verb, B: Preposition, C: Preposition D: Adverb,
E: Preposition

13. A: Pronoun, B: Preposition, C: Preposition, D:
Adjective, E: Verb

14. A: Noun, B: Verb, C: Adjective, D: Adverb, E:
Pronoun

15. A: Adjective, B: Adverb, C: Verb, D: Adjective, E:
Pronoun

Subject-Verb Agreement (p. 18)

1. The process of living vicariously through a fictional character in order to purge one's emotions **is** known as catharsis.

2. Along the border between China and Tibet **lie** the Himalaya Mountains, which include some of the highest peaks in the world.

3. Recognized for formulating unorthodox social theories, Lev Gumilev and D.S. Mirsky **were** partly responsible for founding the neo-eurasianist political and cultural movement.

4. The works of artist Alan Chin **draw** inspiration from both the California gold rush and the construction of the transcontinental railroad

5. Correct

6. Playboating, a discipline of whitewater rafting or canoeing in which players stay in one spot while performing certain maneuvers, **involves** specialized canoes designed for the sport.

7. Often found in plastic drinking bottles **are** substantial amounts of a potentially toxic chemical called Bisphenol A.

8. The African violet, which is known for its striking pink and purple leaves, **belongs** to the Saintpaulia family of flowering plants rather than to the violet family.

9. Among the finds from a recent archaeological dig in London **were** earthenware knobs originally used for "pay walls," boxes into which Elizabethan theater-goers deposited their admission fees.

10. Correct

11. Stiles, structures that **provide** people with a passage through or over a fence, are often built in rural areas or along footpaths.

12. The patent for the first mechanical pencils **was** granted to Sampson Morgan and John Hawkins in England during the early nineteenth century.

13. Each of the Taino's five chiefdoms, which inhabited the Bahamas before the arrival of Europeans, **was** ruled by a leader known as a cacique.

14. If there **are** sufficient funds remaining, the teacher's request for new classroom supplies will most likely be approved by the school board.

15. Possible explanations for the suspicion surrounding Shakespeare's *Macbeth* **include** the superstition that the witches' song is an actual incantation and the belief that theaters only mount the play when they are in need of money.

16. Correct

17. Galaxies, far from being randomly scattered throughout the universe, **appear** to be distributed in bubble-shaped patterns.

18. For the past several years, the theater company **has** traveled to various schools throughout the city in order to expose students to classic works.

19. Over the past several days, a number of disturbing reports **have** filtered in to the news agency, suggesting that the country's government is on the verge of collapse.

20. According to the law of diminution, the pitches of notes sounded by an orchestra **remain** the same even as the amount of sound diminishes.

21. Correct

22. Although the criminal protested his innocence vehemently, neither he nor his lawyer **was** ultimately able to offer a convincing alibi.

23. Sebastian Díaz Morales, like the other members of his generation of artists, **knows** how to draw on the social experiences of his country to produce works that entirely escape any simple interpretation.

24. Historians describe the chariot as a simple type of horse carriage that **was** used by ancient civilizations for peacetime travel and military combat.

25. Along the deepest part of the ocean floor **sit** the Mariana Trench and the HMRG Deep, the two lowest spots that researchers have ever identified on earth.

Present Perfect, Simple Past & Past Perfect (p. 26)

1. Incorrect: allowed

2. Correct

3. Correct

4. Incorrect: had been

5. Correct

6. Incorrect: had been

7. Correct

8. Incorrect: expanded

9. Correct

10. Correct

All Verb Tenses and Forms (p. 27)

1. Correct

2. In 1498, Dutch scholar Erasmus of Rotterdam moved from Paris to England, where he **became** a professor of ancient languages at Cambridge.

3. M.J. Hyland, who authored the acclaimed 2003 novel *How the Light Gets In*, is often praised **as (being)** a subtle and complex portrayer of human psychology.

4. Were an earthquake to strike, the bridge's concrete piers **would** sway and absorb the majority of the shock, limiting damage to areas without extra steel reinforcements.

5. According to researchers, the Antarctic ice shelf has **shrunk** by approximately 50 gigatons of ice each year since 1992.

6. Correct

7. The nearly 200-ton Mayflower was chartered by a group of British merchants and **set** sail from Plymouth, England in 1620.

8. Mahatma Gandhi, who was born in India, studied law in London and in 1893 went to South Africa, where he **spent** twenty years opposing discriminatory legislation against Indians.

9. Accidentally discovered by Procter and Gamble researchers in 1968, the fat substitute Olestra has been shown **to cause** stomach upset in those who consume excessive amounts of it.

10. The country's economists speculated that thousands more jobs would have been lost if consumer demand for domestically manufactured products **had continued** to decline.

11. In the sixteenth century, writer and jurist Noël du Fail **wrote** many stories documenting rural life in France during the Renaissance.

12. Defying predictions that he **would** fade from the public eye, former Czech president Vaclav Havel became a film director after his retirement from office.

13. Descended from a long line of university professors, Marie Goeppert-Mayer received the majority of her training in Germany and eventually **taught** at a number of universities in the United States.

14. After a 1991 attempt to overthrow Mikhail Gorbechav failed, power **shifted** to Russian president Boris Yeltsin.

15. New facts, especially when they replace beliefs already in one's mind, commonly take as long as several weeks **to be** fully accepted as true.

16. Correct

17. The illustrator often photographed multiple models for each drawing and **made** his selection only when the final prints arrived in his hands.

18. Toward the end of the sixteenth century, the Iroquois League, a confederation of six Native American nations, **formed** in the northeastern United States.

19. NASA scientists have decided to delay the space shuttle's launch in order to determine whether recently repaired parts **will** cause damage if they **break** off in orbit. (or: whether repaired parts **would** cause damage if they **broke** off in orbit.)

20. After weeks of careful scrutiny, the consumer protection agency informed the public that a number of products **would** be recalled because of safety concerns.

21. Correct

22. Correct

23. Several dozen boats are known to have **sunk** off of the French Frigate Shoals, part of an enormous protected zone that covers nearly 150,000 square miles in the Pacific Ocean.

24. Emperor Frederick the Great of Prussia believed that to fight a successful war was **to create** minimal intrusion into the lives of civilians.

25. According to cognitive scientist Daniel Willingham, one major reason more students do not enjoy school is that abstract thought is not something our brains are designed to be good at or **to enjoy**.

26. Correct

27. Hardly a stranger to self-censorship, Mark Twain never hesitated to change his prose if he believed that the alterations **would** improve the sales of his books.

28. Some critics have argued that Dostoevsky was unique among nineteenth-century authors in that he surrendered fully to his characters and **allowed** himself to write in voices other than his own.

Pronoun-Antecedent (p. 35)

1. Not until the early twentieth century did the city become capable of maintaining **its** population and cease to be dependent on rural areas for a constant stream of new inhabitants.

2. Correct

3. Pain doesn't show up on a body scan and can't be measured in a test, and as a result, many chronic pain sufferers turn to art in an effort to depict **that sensation/it**.

4. The nitrogen cycle describes **nitrogen's** movement from the air into organic compounds and then back into the atmosphere.

5. If you exercise to prevent diabetes, **you** may want to avoid vitamins C and E since these antioxidants have also been shown to correlate with it.

6. With the price of art lower, collectors for the most part don't want to part with a prized painting or sculpture unless they are forced to do **so**.

7. Once common across southwest Asia, the Indian cheetah was driven nearly to extinction during the late twentieth century and now resides in the fragmented pieces of **its** remaining suitable habitat.

8. Although Alice Sebold does not write her books with any particular age group in mind, **they have** proven popular with middle and high school students.

9. Some critics of the Internet have argued that it is a danger to people because its vastness, often heralded as a benefit, threatens **their** intellectual health.

10. The woolly mammoth and the saber-toothed tiger might have survived as late as 10,000 B.C., although **they** went extinct fairly abruptly right around that time.

11. When the auditorium closes next year for renovations, the theater company will probably hold **its** productions at another location.

12. Correct

13. One measure of a society's openness to newcomers is the quality of the space **it** creates for people of unfamiliar cultural and linguistic backgrounds.

14. Though recipes for yeast-free muffins were commonly found in nineteenth-century cookbooks, by the twentieth century most muffin recipes were calling for **yeast**.

15. Correct

16. The Egyptian temple complex at Karnak, situated on the eastern bank of the Nile, was the **Egyptian's** sacred place of worship.

17. The city's economy has weakened significantly over the past decade, **leading/a situation that has led** to an overwhelming loss of manufacturing jobs.

18. In the announcement, the school committee stated that **it** would substantially overhaul the eleventh grade curriculum at some point during the next year.

19. The world's population could climb to 10.5 billion by 2050, **raising/a statistic that raises** questions about how many people the Earth can support.

20. Paul and Julio had just returned from a long and exhausting hike along the Appalachian Trail when **Paul/Julio** stumbled and hit his head.

21. In order to become truly great at a sport, players must spend most of **their** free time practicing.

22. Japan's status as an island country means that **the Japanese** must rely heavily on other countries for the supply of natural resources that are indispensable to national existence.

23. The Marquesa islands were among the first South Pacific islands to be settled, and from **their** shores departed some of the greatest navigators of all time.

24. Google's dominance as an Internet search function has allowed the company to expand **its** ambitions to include virtually all aspects of the online world.

25. Correct

Pronoun Case (p. 40)

1. Although our parents have little difficulty distinguishing between my twin sister and **me**, our teachers are much more easily fooled by our seemingly identical appearance.

2. For **us** voters, it is exceedingly difficult to choose between the two candidates because their positions on so many issues are so similar that they are virtually indistinguishable.

3. After listening patiently to our admittedly flimsy excuses, the principal decided to sentence Akiko and **me** to a week of detention.

4. Along with our project, the professor handed Shalini and **me** a note requesting that we remain after class in order to discuss our research methods with her.

5. Correct

6. Correct

7. When the gubernatorial candidate arrived at the auditorium to give a speech, we found it nearly impossible to distinguish between **her** and her assistant, so similar were they in height and appearance.

8. My lab partner and **I** were awarded first prize in the science fair for our work on the breakdown of insulin production in people who suffer from diabetes.

9. Walking through Yellowstone National Park, Jordan, Sam, and **I** were so astonished by our surroundings that we found ourselves at a loss for words.

10. An unfamiliar subject when the class began, Roman history became increasingly fascinating to **him** and Alexis over the course of the semester.

Cumulative Review #1 (p. 41)

1. The works of Paulus Barbus **have** largely been lost, although many editions of his works were both published and esteemed during the Renaissance.

2. Among the writings of linguist Margaret Landon **were** a dictionary of the Native American Degueño dialect and a comparative study of Central American languages.

3. Many runners, even those who train regularly, do not have a clear sense of their potential since **they tend** to stick to an established distance.

4. For centuries, Norwegians **have hung** dolls dressed as witches in their kitchens because they believe that such figures have the power to keep pots from burning over.

5. When the fossil of an enormous ancient penguin was unearthed in Peru, archaeologists discovered that **its** feathers were brown and gray rather than black and white.

6. Although the waiter offered to bring Ramon and **me** a list of desserts, we had already eaten too much and found the prospect of more food unappetizing.

7. At the meeting point of the Alaskan and the Aleutian mountains **rise** an immense alpine tundra and sparkling lakes, which give way to thundering waterfalls.

8. Since 1896, the Kentucky Derby – arguably the best-known horse race in America – has **taken** place on a track measuring one-and-a-quarter miles.

9. Sultan Suleyman I, known as Suleyman the Magnificent, **was** responsible for the expansion of the Ottoman Empire from Asia Minor to North Africa before his death in 1566.

10. Long Island was the setting for F. Scott Fitzgerald's novel *The Great Gatsby*, but finding traces of **it/the book/the characters** there is as much a job for the imagination as it is for a map and a guidebook.

11. Correct

12. People who seek out extreme sports such as skydiving and mountain climbing often do so because **they** feel compelled to explore the limits of their endurance.

13. While **you are** cooking a recipe that involves large quantities of hot chili peppers, you should generally try to avoid touching your eyes.

14. Chicago's Sears Tower was the tallest office building in the world for nearly thirty years, a distinction it **lost** only upon the completion of the Taipei 101 Tower in 2004.

15. Born in Spain in 1881, Pablo Picasso **would** become one of the most celebrated and revolutionary painters of the twentieth century because of his invention of the cubist style.

16. The Sherlock Holmes form of mystery novel, which **revolves** around a baffling crime solved by a master detective and his assistant, contrasts the scientific method with prevailing superstitions.

17. In the early years of the fourteenth century, Pope Clement V moved the papacy to the French city of Avignon and **left** Rome prey to the ambitions of local overlords.

18. Correct

19. Although the two books recount the same series of events, they do **so** from different perspectives and are not intended to be read in any particular order.

20. Roberta and her supervisor, Ms. Altschuler, were commended at the company's dinner for **Roberta's (or: Ms. Alschuler's)** exceptional performance during the previous year.

21. Correct

22. South Africa experienced a series of massive and devastating blackouts in 2008, and consequently **it has** been rationing electricity ever since that time.

23. Though extremely long, the meeting between my advisor and **me** was unusually productive because it provided me with many new ways of thinking about a familiar subject.

24. Although prairie dogs were once on the verge of extinction, their numbers have **risen** to pre-twentieth century levels because of the work of the environmentalists who lobbied for their salvation.

25. In response **to being** criticized for the poor nutritional value of its food, the restaurant chain has altered its menu to include more healthful options.

Adjectives vs. Adverbs (p. 45)

1. Correct

2. Explorers who arrived at the central stretch of the Nile River **excitedly** reported the discovery of elegant temples and pyramids, ruins of the ancient Kushite civilization.

3. By looking **closely** at DNA markers, scientists may have found traces of the first African hunter-gatherers to migrate to other continents.

4. Although the room appeared tidy at first glance, I saw upon closer inspection that books, pens, and pieces of paper had been scattered **haphazardly** beneath a desk.

5. When examined under a microscope, the beaker of water revealed a hodgepodge of microscopic drifters that looked quite **different** from other sea creatures.

6. When Mt. Vesuvius first began to show signs of eruption, many of the people living at the base of the volcano **hastily** abandoned their villages to seek cover in nearby forests.

7. The archaeologists were lauded for their discovery of the ancient city, once a **densely** populated urban area that profited from the trade of precious metals.

8. Correct

9. Italian nobleman Cesare Borgia was ruthless and vain, but he was also a brilliant Renaissance man who was **exceedingly** well-educated in the classics.

10. Though few people believe that human beings are entirely rational, a world governed by anti-Enlightenment principles would surely be **infinitely** worse than one governed by Voltaire and Locke.

11. Lake Pergusa, the only **naturally** occurring lake in Sicily, is surrounded by a well-known racing circuit that was created in the 1960's and that has hosted many international sporting events since that time.

12. Even when his theme is the struggle to find a place in a **seemingly** irrational cosmos, Oscar Wilde writes with lively sympathy and hopefulness.

Parallel Structure I: Lists (p. 47)

1. Lady Jane Grey, known as the nine-day queen, was renowned for her sweetness, her beauty, and **her subjection to** the whims of her mother.

2. Mediterranean cooking is best known for its reliance on fresh produce, whole grains, **and significant amounts** of olive oil.

3. Correct

4. The term "single family house" describes how a house is built and who is intended to live in it, but it does not indicate the house's size, shape, or **location**.

5. Seeing the Grand Canyon, standing in front of a beautiful piece of art, and **listening** to a beautiful symphony are all experiences that may inspire awe.

6. Neighbors of the proposed park argue that an amphitheater would draw more traffic, disrupt their neighborhood, and **diminish** their only patch of open space.

7. Evidence suggests that the aging brain retains and even increases its capacity for resilience, growth, and **well-being**.

8. Antiques are typically objects that show some degree of craftsmanship or attention to design, and they are considered desirable because of their beauty, rarity, or **usefulness**.

9. Spiders use a wide range of strategies to capture prey, including trapping it in sticky webs, lassoing it with sticky bolas, and **mimicking** other insects in order to avoid detection.

10. According to medical authorities at the Mayo Clinic, building muscle can boost metabolism, **aid** in weight loss, and increase stamina and focus.

Prepositions and Idioms (p. 50)

1. The Wave, a sandstone rock formation located near the Utah-Arizona border, is famous **for** its colorful outcroppings and rugged, unpaved trails.

2. Frank Lloyd Wright was a proponent **of** organic architecture, a philosophy that he incorporated into structures such as the Fallingwater residence.

3. Correct

4. As an old man, Rousseau acknowledged that it was arrogant of him to promote virtues that he was unable to embody **in** his own life.

5. Correct

6. Beethoven, who strongly sympathized **with** the ideals of the French Revolution, originally planned to name the *Eroica* symphony after Napoleon.

7. Choreographer Alvin Ailey Jr. is credited **with** popularizing modern dance and integrating traditional African movements into his works.

8. As a result of its new program, which consists **of** three world premiers, the ballet troupe has become one of the few eminent companies to promote choreographic innovation.

9. **Unlike/In contrast to** his contemporaries, whose work he viewed as conventional and uninspiring, Le Corbusier insisted on using modern industrial techniques to construct buildings.

10. Both bizarre and familiar, fairy tales are intended to be spoken aloud rather than read, and they truly possess an inexhaustible power **over** children and adults alike.

11. Correct

12. Teachers have begun to note with alarm that the amount of time their students spend playing video games and surfing the Internet has severely impacted their ability to focus **on** a single task for an extended period of time.

13. During the early decades of the Heian Empire, a person who lacked a thorough knowledge **of** Chinese could never be considered fully educated.

14. Correct

15. In "Howl" as well as in his other poetry, Allen Ginsberg drew inspiration from the epic, free verse style associated **with** the nineteenth century poet Walt Whitman.

Faulty Comparisons (p. 53)

1. The writings of John Locke, unlike **those of** Thomas Hobbes, emphasize the idea that people are by nature both reasonable and tolerant.

2. Company officials announced that there would be no major changes made to the eligibility requirements for its benefits package, an offering that makes its plan more generous than **those of** other major retailers.

3. As part of its application, the university asks students to compose a short essay in which they compare their educational interests and goals to **those of** other students.

4. The humor in Lynne Shelton's film *Touchy Feely* is softer and more ambiguous than **that of/in** her earlier films, and its characters' transformations are sharper and more difficult to comprehend.

5. Unlike **people/those with** dyslexia, people with dysgraphia often suffer from fine motor-skills problems that leave them unable to write clearly.

6. Today's neuroscientists, unlike **those of** thirty years ago, have access to sophisticated instrumentation that has only been developed over the past decade.

7. Norwegian doctors prescribe fewer antibiotics than **those of** any other country, so people do not have a chance to develop resistance to many kinds of drug-resistant infections.

8. Correct

9. The reproduction of ciliates, unlike **that of other organisms**, occurs when a specimen splits in half and grows a completely new individual from each piece.

10. The hands and feet of Ardi, the recently discovered human ancestor who lived 4.4 million years ago, are much like **those of** other primitive extinct apes.

11. At the age of twenty-four, playwright Thornton Wilder was balding and bespectacled, and his clothes were like **those of** a much older man.

12. In ancient Greece, women were not allowed to vote or hold property, their status differing from **that of** slaves only in name.

Word Pairs (p. 56)

1. Known for his designs inspired by natural principles, architect Michael Pawlyn was initially torn between architecture **and** biology but eventually chose the former.

2. After weeks of unproductive negotiations, workers have finally agreed to discuss the overtime dispute with both outside mediators **and** company officials.

3. Once stereotyped as savants because of their depictions in movies such as *Rain Man*, people on the autistic spectrum are typically neither superhuman memory machines **nor** incapable of performing everyday tasks.

4. Obedience to authority is not only a way for rulers to keep order in totalitarian states **but also** the foundation on which such states exist.

5. Correct

6. Audiences find the play at once amusing because of the comedic skills of its leading actors **and** tedious because of its excessive length.

7. It is almost as difficult to find consistent information about the Fort Pillow incident during the American Civil War **as** it is to determine the significance of its outcome.

8. Correct

9. Because the Articles of Confederation did not provide for the creation of either executive agencies **or** judiciary institutions, they were rejected in favor of the Constitution.

10. Correct

11. One of the main effects of industrialization was the shift from a society in which women worked at home **to** one in which women worked in factories and brought home wages to their families.

12. Over the past decade, Internet usage has become so pervasive **that** many psychologists are beginning to study its effects on the lives of children and adolescents.

13. It was not until the late seventeenth century **that** some English writers began to challenge the traditional view of commerce, which held that money-making was a source of moral corruption to be avoided at all cost.

14. Correct

15. Although Voltaire wrote a number of tragedies and believed he would be remembered as a dramatist, he is known today not so much for his theatrical works **as** for his satires.

Cumulative Review #2 (p. 57)

1. Three million years ago, the creation of the Panama Isthmus wreaked ecological havoc by triggering extinctions, diverting ocean currents, and **transforming** the climate. (Parallel Structure)

2. The professor's appearance was very striking to everyone in the room, for not only was he extremely thin, but his height also surpassed **that of** a normal man. (Faulty Comparison)

3. Although many children want to read digitized books and would read for fun more **frequently** if they could obtain them, most claim that do not want to give up traditional print books completely. (Adjective vs. Adverb)

4. Correct

5. Although clarinetist Artie Shaw spent far more of his long life writing prose than making music, a careful look at his compositions **reveals** that he was a musician of genius. (Subject-Verb Agreement: Subject–Prepositional Phrase–Verb)

6. Among the earliest complex civilizations in Mexico **was** the Olmec culture which flourished on the gulf coast from around 1500 BCE. (Subject-Verb Agreement: Prepositional Phrase–Verb–Subject)

7. Although the movie has alternately been described as a social satire, a comedy of manners, and **a Greek tragedy**, it contains elements of all three. (Parallel Structure)

8. In the early nineteenth century, a number of adventurous artists and writers flocked to Lake Geneva to **savor its** inspiring mountain scenery and serene atmosphere. (Preposition)

9. Parrots are not only capable of mimicking human speech in some cases also demonstrate the ability to form associations between words **and** their meanings. (Word Pair: between…and)

10. *The Europeans*, a short novel by Henry James, contrasts the behavior and attitudes of two visitors from Italy with **those of** their cousins from New England. (Faulty Comparison)

11. Thomas Jefferson believed that prisoners of war should be treated **humanely** and, during the American Revolution, requested that British and Hessian generals be held in mansions rather than behind bars. (Adjective vs. Adverb)

12. Correct

13. A rebellion **against** the rigid academic art that predominated during the nineteenth century, the Art Nouveau movement was inspired by natural forms and structures. (Preposition)

14. Although the best-selling author had **grown** comfortable with her role as a public figure, when given the choice, she preferred to be alone. (Tense: Past Participle vs. Simple Past)

15. While reactions to the exhibition were mixed, neither the artist's exceptional showmanship nor his astonishing technique **was** questioned by the spectators. (Subject-Verb Agreement: Neither…Nor)

16. Unlike **those of (or: the novels of)** Nathaniel Hawthorne and F. Scott Fitzgerald, Jonathan Franzen's novels have not yet received unanimous acceptance as classic works of literature. (Faulty Comparison)

17. Supporters of bilingual education often imply that students miss a great deal by not **being** taught in the language spoken by their parents and siblings at home. (Gerund vs. Infinitive)

18. A small frontier town in the 1830's, Chicago had grown to more than two million residents by 1909, and some demographers predicted that it **would** soon be the largest city on earth. (Tense: Would vs. Will)

19. John Breckinridge, who came closest **to** defeating Abraham Lincoln in the 1860 election, held strong personal convictions that made it difficult for him to navigate a moderate course in an era of extremes. (Preposition)

20. According to many urban planners, the most efficient way of building prosperous cities is to make **them** not only attractive but also healthy. (Pronoun-Antecedent)

21. The origin of the senators' proposal dates to the mid-twentieth century, making it one of the most **eagerly** anticipated pieces of legislation this year. (Adjective vs. Adverb)

22. Societies located at river deltas tend to foster innovation because of their flexibility **in dealing** with potentially shifting landscapes. (Gerund vs. Infinitive)

23. Correct

24. Correct

25. Correct

Noun Agreement (p. 60)

1. Both Wilfrid Daniels and Leonard Chuene, now powerful figures in South African sports, grew up as promising **athletes** who could never compete internationally because of apartheid.

2. Because they evolved in the warm climate of Africa before spreading into Europe, modern humans had **bodies** adapted to tracking prey over great distances.

3. Many of the great classical composers, including Mozart, Bach, and Mendelssohn, were born into musical families and began studying music seriously when they were **children**.

4. Correct

5. Known for creating a unique sound and style through the use of non-traditional instruments such as the French horn, Miles Davis joined Louis Armstrong and Ella Fitzgerald **as one of** the greatest jazz musicians of the twentieth century.

6. Inscribed ostrich eggs and pieces of shell jewelry are **examples** of early human attempts to record thoughts symbolically rather than literally.

7. Joseph Charles Jones and George Bundy Smith, who fought for African-Americans as **civil rights activists** during the early 1960's, were separated for nearly forty years after being arrested in Alabama in 1961.

8. The Opium Wars, which introduced the power of western armies and technologies to China, marked the end of Shanghai and Ningpo as independent **port cities**.

9. Although neither came from a literary family, Amy Tan and Maxine Hong Kingston became **avid readers** while growing up near San Francisco.

10. Correct

Comparatives vs. Superlatives (p. 62)

1. Between the black leopard and the snow leopard, the black leopard possesses the more effective camouflage while the snow leopard has the **more** striking tail.

2. Correct

3. Correct

4. While triathlons, competitions that consist of swimming, biking, and running, are drawing increasing numbers of participants, athletic events devoted to a single sport remain **more** popular.

5. Correct

6. Confronted with two equally qualified finalists, the awards committee is struggling to determine which one is **more** deserving of the top prize.

7. Correct

8. Though London has a longstanding reputation as a city's whose weather is defined by rain and fog, in reality Paris receives the **higher** amount of rainfall each year.

9. Both poodles and pugs are known for making excellent pets, but between the two breeds, pugs have the **sweeter** disposition while poodles are smarter.

10. Although mental puzzles such as Sudoku can help people keep their minds nimble as they age, physical exercise such as biking or running is **more** effective.

Relative Pronouns (p. 65)

1. For delicate patients **who** cannot handle the rigors of modern medicine, some doctors are now rejecting the assembly line of modern medical care for older, gentler options.

2. Correct

3. When readers **who** get their news from electronic rather than printed sources send articles to their friends, they tend to choose ones that contain intellectually challenging topics.

4. In 1623, Galileo published a work **in which** he championed the controversial theory of heliocentrism, thus provoking one of the greatest scientific controversies of his day.

5. In classical Athenian democracy, citizens **who** failed to pay their debts were barred from attending assembly meetings and appearing in court in virtually any capacity.

6. Correct

7. Researchers have claimed that subjects **who** stood on a rapidly vibrating platform during an experiment were able to slightly improve their athletic performance for a short time afterward.

8. Correct.

9. One of the least popular of all the Romance languages, Romansch is traditionally spoken by people **who** inhabit the southern regions of Switzerland.

10. Correct

Double Negatives and Double Positives (p. 67)

1. When selecting a host city from among dozens of contenders, Olympic officials must take into consideration which one is **likeliest** to benefit from the legacy of the games.

2. Although the plays of Lillian Hellman and Bertolt Brecht were met with great popularity during the 1920's, they are scarcely **ever** performed anymore in the United States.

3. Since the advent of commercial flight and high-speed rail in the twentieth century, hardly **any** significant technological change has affected the traveling public.

4. An evolutionary adaptation that might have promised survival during prehistoric times is **likelier** nowadays to produce diseases in modern humans.

5. Correct

6. The Indian sub-continent was home to some of the **earliest** civilizations, ranging from urban society of the Indus Valley to the classical age of the Gupta Dynasty.

7. During the early days of cable television, many viewers were only able to access four channels, with reception being weakest in rural areas and **clearest** in large cities.

8. The Industrial Revolution, which began in the late 1700's and lasted more than fifty years, was the period when machine power became **stronger** than hand power.

9. Correct

10. To thoroughly understand historical figures, we must study them not only in the bright light of the present but also in the **cloudier** light of the circumstances they encountered in their own lifetimes.

Conjunctions (p. 71)

1. In the past, coffees were blended and branded to suit a homogenous popular taste, **but** that has recently changed in response to a growing awareness of regional differences.

2. Frederic Chopin's charming and sociable personality drew loyal groups of friends and admirers, including George Sand, **but** his private life was often painful and difficult.

3. The Taj Mahal is regarded as one of the eight wonders of the world, **and** some historians have noted that its architectural beauty has never been surpassed.

4. Music serves no obvious evolutionary purpose, **but** it has been, and remains, part of every known civilization on earth.

5. Correct

6. Saving an endangered species requires preservationists to study it in detail, **but** unfortunately scientific information about some animals is scarce. (Or: **Although** saving an endangered species requires preservationists to study it in detail, unfortunately scientific information about some animals is scarce.)

7. Correct

8. Modern chemistry keeps insects from ravaging crops, lifts stains from carpets, and saves lives, **but** the constant exposure to chemicals is taking a toll on many people's health.

9. If people were truly at home under the light of the moon and stars, they would go in darkness happily, **but** their eyes are adapted to the sun's light.

10. Correct

11. Roman women could only exercise political power through men, the only people considered true citizens, **for/because** they were not allowed to participate directly in politics.

Cumulative Review #3 (p. 72)

1. In their stories, originally published in the eighteenth century, the Brothers Grimm **embraced** a number of themes that have never vanished from life, despite modern advances in science and technology. (Tense Consistency: Present Perfect vs. Simple Past)

2. Correct

3. Entomologists have identified the jewel beetle and the fire-chaser beetle as **insects** that can thrive in trees scorched by wildfires or destroyed by other natural disasters. (Noun Agreement)

4. Objectivity, one of the central values of science, is based on the idea that scientists must aspire to eliminate all **their** personal biases in attempting to uncover truths about the natural world. (Pronoun-Antecedent)

5. A recently undertaken survey of drivers and cyclists has revealed that, compared to drivers, cyclists are **more** likely to use hand signals. (Comparative vs. Superlative)

6. Lan Samantha Chang is a critically acclaimed novelist **who** counts among her influences authors as varied as Charlotte Brontë and Edgar Allan Poe. (Who vs. Which)

7. In response to their critics, advocates of genetically modified foods typically insist that such crops grow faster, require fewer pesticides, and **reduce** stress on natural resources. (Parallel Structure)

8. Much like human beings, wolves are capable of exerting a profound influence on the environments that **they** inhabit. (Pronoun-Antecedent)

9. Giant galaxies like the Milky Way and the nearby Andromeda galaxy, which is even **larger**, possess the power to create and retain a wide variety of elements. (Double Positive)

10. Many scientists are baffled **by** the appearance of Yersinia pestis, a fungus that has been destroying bat populations throughout the United States in recent years. (Preposition)

11. Migrating animals maintain a fervid attentiveness that allows them to be **neither** distracted by temptations **nor** deterred by challenges that would turn other animals aside. (Word Pair)

12. Correct

13. Dumping pollution in oceans **not only** adds to the unsightliness of the formerly pristine waters **but it also** destroys the marine life that inhabits them. (Word Pair)

14. Correct

15. When it was first built, the Spanish Armada was said to be invincible, a designation that quickly became ironic since it was destroyed by the British in **hardly any** time. (Double Negative)

16. Correct

17. Construction on the Great Wall of China began many thousands of years ago and initially **involved** the creation of hundreds of miles of fortresses to defend against foreign invaders. (Tense Consistency)

18. The earliest surviving guitars date from the sixteenth century, **but** images of guitar-like instruments were depicted in Egyptian paintings and murals as early as 1900 B.C. (Conjunction)

19. The women in the nearly century-old photograph seemed strangely familiar to Shayla and **me**, but try as we might, we could not recall where we had seen them before. (Pronoun Case)

20. A new generation of powerful digital tools and databases **is** transforming the study of literature, philosophy and other humanistic fields. (Subject-Verb Agreement: Subject-Prepositional Phrase-Verb)

21. Correct

22. Well into the twentieth century, to defend the notion of full social and political equality for all members of society was **to be** considered a fool. (Verb Consistency; Gerund vs. Infinitive)

23. Although George Washington and General Lafayette were great friends, they came from **widely** disparate backgrounds and had little in common. (Adjective vs. Adverb)

24. Correct

25. Although birds are not generally known for their intelligence, recent findings have established that parrots often possess skills similar to **those of** human toddlers. (Faulty Comparison)

Redundancy (p. 75)

1. *Glengarry Glen Ross* earned David Mamet a Pulitzer Prize in 1984, eight years after a trio of off-Broadway plays **initially** garnered him major acclaim **for the first time**.

2. Although the students in the auditorium were silent throughout the entire lecture, the professor spoke so softly that his voice was **nearly inaudible** and **could hardly be heard**.

3. Scuba divers usually move around underwater by using fins attached to their feet, but **external** propulsion can be provided **from an outside source** by a specialized propulsion vehicle or a sled pulled from the surface.

4. Accused of purposefully neglecting to follow crucial steps in the laboratory's safety protocol, the researcher insisted that the oversight was **inadvertent** and had occurred **entirely by accident**.

5. Faced with reports of a breaking scandal, company executives **deliberately** concealed the news from both shareholders and consumers **on purpose** because they feared the inevitable financial consequences.

6. Both the raw ingredients and distillation technology used by early perfumers **significantly influenced** the development of chemistry, on which it **had an important effect**.

7. Although the city of Troy, described by Homer in *The Illiad*, was long believed to be an **imaginary** city that **did not exist**, recent excavations have revealed remains consistent with some of the locations depicted in the book.

8. Vietnam became independent from Imperial China in 938 AD following the Battle of Bach Dang River, with **consecutive** Vietnamese royal dynasties flourishing **one after the other** as the nation expanded geographically and politically into Southeast Asia.

9. No error

10. **Historically**, only a small group of educated elites were taught to write **in the past**, so written records tend to reflect the assumptions and values of a limited range of individuals.

Diction (p. 77)

1. To attract **prospective** students, the university has planned a series of lectures and open houses designed to exhibit its wide variety of academic programs and newly renovated facilities.

2. Since its publication last year, the biography has earned **unanimous** praise, with everyone from casual readers to established critics agreeing that it is one of the best books of its kind in recent memory.

3. During the trial, the defense attorney argued that the police's repeated questioning of the suspect without a lawyer present represented a clear **violation** of his client's rights.

4. Large fires, far from destroying forests, can act as catalysts that **stimulate** biodiversity and promote ecological health throughout an ecosystem.

5. When she returned home from the library, Ines was surprised to discover that her wallet was missing because she was not at all **conscious** of having dropped anything as she walked.

6. The physics professor was awarded the university's top teaching award because of her ability to make a difficult subject unusually **comprehensible** to her students.

7. No error

8. The biologists wore masks as well as gloves during their **descent** into the cave because it was believed to be a natural reservoir for several highly infectious diseases.

9. A dog's ears are far more **sensitive** than those of a human: they pick up frequencies at more than twice the range that human ears can perceive.

10. Although the fugitive managed to **elude** capture for several weeks, he was finally caught after his picture was displayed on national television for several consecutive days.

Practice Error-Identifications (p. 85)

1. B: Adjective vs. Adverb

Blessed with an **exceptionally** rugged natural landscape, New Zealand has drawn thrill-seeking athletes in search of adventure for decades.

2. D: Pronoun-Antecedent

Franz Kafka's novel *The Trial* opens with the unexplained arrest of Josef K. by a mysterious organization that runs **its** courts outside the normal criminal-justice system.

Clue: The word "organization" is a collective noun, which points to either a subject-verb agreement or a pronoun-antecedent error

3. E: Correct

Clue: The prepositional phrase ("in a trunk") that appears at the beginning of the sentence suggests that this is a Prepositional Phrase–Verb–Subject error. The fact that this error does not then appear indicates that the correct answer is likely to be (E).

Error-Identification Test (p. 88)

1. C: Tense Consistency

The Last Five years, a musical written by Jason Robert Brown, premiered in Chicago in 2001 and **was** produced numerous times both in the United States and internationally.

2. D: Parallel Structure

Among the many reasons healthcare professionals choose jobs that require travel are higher pay, professional growth and development, and **opportunity for** personal adventures. (suggested)

3. B: Subject-Verb Agreement: Subject–Non-Essential Clause–Verb

The tower of London, which lies within the Borough of Tower Hamlets, **is** separated from the city itself by a stretch of open space.

4. A: Who vs. Which

Originally a common breakfast eaten by farmers **who** lived in the canton of Bern, rösti is today considered the unofficial national dish of Switzerland.

5. D: Adjective vs. Adverb

The Australian frilled lizard responds to attacks by unfurling the colorful skin flap that encircles its head, but if all else fails it will scoot **nimbly** up the nearest tree.

6. D: Would vs. Will

Sofia Tolstoy, the wife of Russian author Leo Tolstoy, was a woman of strength and spirit who understood the high price she **would** pay to live next to one of the greatest writers in history.

7. B: Noun Agreement

James Watson and Francis Crick were renowned as **scientists** because they discovered the DNA triple helix and in 1962 were awarded the Nobel Prize in Medicine.

8. B: Word Pair

Among nations known for producing exceptional chess players, **neither** China **nor** Russia can compete with Armenia for the sheer number of grandmasters it has produced.

9. A: Double Positive

Humor is a far **subtler** process than a primeval pleasure such as eating, but it is just as much tied to the inner complexity of the brain.

10. E: No Error

11. D: Pronoun-Antecedent

The secret of the Mona Lisa's enigmatic smile is a matter of which cells in the retina pick up the image and how **they channel** the information to the brain.

12. B: Tense Consistency/Past Perfect

Located on the outskirts of Lincoln National Forest in New Mexico, White Oaks **became** a boomtown following the discovery silver and gold in the nearby Jicarilla Mountains in 1879.

13. A: Preposition

The Ethiopian wolf, the only species of wolf native **to** Africa, can be identified by its distinctive red coat and black-and-white tail.

14. C: Gerund vs. Infinitive

Far from eliminating war, the new diplomatic system instituted in Europe during the early nineteenth century simply changed the reasons **for fighting** and the means of combat.

15. A: Faulty Comparison

With genes that are virtually identical to **those of** humans, Neanderthals can offer many insights into the evolution and development of the modern brain.

16. A: Subject-Verb Agreement (Subject–Prepositional Phrase–Verb)

The popularity of games such as cricket and squash in former English colonies **is** often attributed to the lingering influence of British culture.

17. E: No Error

Sentences and Fragments (p. 96)

1. Shirley Jackson, best known for her shocking short story **"The Lottery," was** born in San Francisco in 1916.

2. Correct

3. The pyramids of ancient Egypt, intended to be monuments to the Pharaohs' **greatness, were** built with the help of great armies of slaves.

4. The Red **Belt, (which was) one of** several colored belts used in some martial arts to denote a practitioner's skill level and rank, originated in Japan and Korea.

5. The plan to overhaul the country's higher education system **is** a model for moving other desperately needed projects forward.

6. Correct

7. Recent findings from research on moose **have suggested** that arthritis in human beings may be linked in part to nutritional deficits.

8. A new study **reports** that the physical differences among dog breeds are determined by variations in only about seven genetic regions.

9. George Barr McCutcheon, a popular novelist and **playwright, is** best known for the series of novels set in Graustark, a fictional Eastern European country.

10. Forensic biology, **(which is) the application** of biology to law enforcement, has been used to identify illegal products from endangered species and investigate bird collisions with wind turbines.

11. Human computers, who once performed basic numerical analysis for **laboratories, were** behind the calculations for everything from the first accurate prediction of the return of Halley's Comet to the success of the Manhattan Project.

12. Nicollet Island, an island in the Mississippi River just north of **Minneapolis, was** named after cartographer Joseph Nicollet.

13. Malba Tahan, (who was) a fictitious Persian **scholar, was** the pen name created by Brazilian author Julio Cesar de Mello e Souza.

14. The Rochester International Jazz Festival **takes** place in June of each year and typically attracts more than 100,000 fans from towns across upstate New York.

15. Although Rodin purposely omitted crucial elements such as arms from his sculptures, his consistent use of the human figure **attested** to his respect for artistic tradition.

16. Brick nog **is** a commonly used construction technique in which one width of bricks is used to fill the vacancies in a wooden frame.

17. The unusually large size of the komodo dragon, the largest species of **lizard, has** been attributed to its ancient ancestor, the immense varanid lizard.

18. Correct

19. One of the most popular ballets, *Swan Lake*, which was fashioned from Russian folk tales, **tells** the story of Odette, a princess turned into a swan by an evil sorcerer's curse.

20. Pheidon, a king of the Greek city Argos during the seventh century **B.C., ruled** during a time when monarchs were figureheads with little genuine power.

21. Batsford Arboretum, a 55-acre garden that contains Great Britain's largest collection of Japanese cherry **trees, is** open daily to the public for most of the year.

Is it a Sentence? (p. 102)

1. Independent

2. Independent

3. Independent

4. Independent

5. Independent

6. Independent

7. Independent

8. Dependent

9. Independent

10. Dependent

Commas and Semicolons (p. 108)

1. In large doses, many common substances found in household items have devastating **effects; however,** many toxicologists insist that they are thoroughly innocuous in minuscule amounts.

2. Correct

3. Correct

4. African-American life during the 1920s was documented in great detail by the writers and artists of the Harlem **Renaissance; far** less is known about it during the 1930s.

5. Universities have historically offered a wide variety of continuing education classes, many of **which (or: many of** them) are now offered over the Internet as well as in traditional classrooms.

6. When the Mayan city of Palenque was first discovered, it was overwhelmed by the plant life of the **rain forest; today** it is a massive archaeological site that attracts thousands of tourists each year.

7. The geologic instability known as the Pacific Ring of Fire has produced numerous **faults, which** cause **(or: faults, causing)** approximately 10,000 earthquakes annually.

8. Correct

9. The First World War began in August of **1914; it** was directly caused by the assassination of Archduke Franz Ferdinand of Austria by Bosnian revolutionary Gavrilo Princeps.

10. Correct

11. Correct

12. The black-backed woodpecker lives almost exclusively in severely burned **forests; it** thrives on insects that are adapted to fire and can detect heat up to 30 miles away.

13. International sports competitions are symbolic showdowns that are more about winning than about universal **friendship; however,** they are a far more civilized alternative to actual warfare.

14. Culture has become a force that may accelerate human **evolution because** people have no choice but to adapt to pressures and technologies of their own creation.

15. Found in the depths of all the world's oceans, the vampire squid lives in a twilight zone that that contains extremely low levels of dissolved **oxygen; most** other sea creatures cannot inhabit such regions.

16. Correct

17. Paris is known as a world capital of **movie-making; moreover,** the city itself has played a central role in films of every imaginable genre.

18. Sugar and cavities go hand in **hand; therefore,** dentists recommend that the amount of sugar people consume be kept to a minimum.

19. Correct

20. The Mid-Autumn Festival, a popular harvest festival celebrated in Asia, dates back 3,000 years to China's Shang **Dynasty and** is traditionally held on the fifteenth day of the eighth month.

21. Carl Bohm was one of the most prolific German pianists and composers during the nineteenth **century; few** people would, however, recognize his name today.

22. Correct

23. Despite strains, fractures and tears, many athletes continue to work **out; consequently,** at least one expert would say that they are addicted to exercise.

24. Frederick Law Olmsted, who designed New York's Central Park, also designed Montreal's Mount Royal Park, most of **which** is heavily wooded.

25. During the nineteenth century, Detroit's road transportation and railways system were **improved; nevertheless,** the city's manufacturing sector remained weak until after the Industrial Revolution.

Gerunds and Wordiness (p. 113)

1. It can hardly be considered a surprise that Incan emperors covered themselves in gold **because they held** themselves to be the sun's human incarnation.

2. The museum's artistic director has arranged the exhibition thematically **in order to provide** a new understanding of the multifaceted complexity of Native American life.

3. Correct

4. **Although it is** a smaller city than either London or New York, Dublin possesses a thriving theater scene whose productions regularly achieve international renown.

5. Correct

6. Bongoyo Island, located off the coast of Tanzania, has become a popular vacation spot for both tourists and Tanzanians **because it has** such close proximity to the mainland.

7. The Province House, home to royal governors in seventeenth-century Massachusetts, was considered one of the grandest examples of colonial architecture **because it possessed** beautiful Tudor-style chimneystacks.

8. Contrary to popular belief, people should alternate rooms while studying **because they retain** more information that way.

9. Some excellent teachers prance in front of the classroom like Shakespearean actors, while others are notable **because they are** aloof or timid.

10. Correct

11. *Prince Jellyfish*, an unpublished novel by author and journalist Hunter S. Thompson, was rejected by a number of literary agents **because it lacked** popular appeal.

12. Correct

13. **Although traffic often blocks** its main arteries, East London contains side streets that can, on occasion, be as tranquil and pleasant as country lanes.

14. In scientific fields, scale models known as homunculi are often used **to illustrate** physiological characteristics of the human body.

Passive Voice (p. 115)

1. In the later works of Nikola Stoyanov, also known by the pseudonym Emiliyan Stanev, the author often describes nature in great detail.

2. Michael J. Rosen has written works ranging from picture books to poetry, and he has also edited several anthologies varying almost as broadly in content.

3. In the movie *The Killing Fields*, first-time actor Haing S. Ngor portrayed Cambodian photojournalist Dith Pran, a role for which Ngor won an Academy Award.

4. Although desserts **are** typically characterized by their sweetness, bakers are now creating ones that feature intriguing blends of sweet and savory.

5. Scientists at the Woods Hole Oceanographic Institute designed *The Nereus*, a remotely operated underwater hybrid vehicle, to function at depths of up to 36,000 feet.

6. Many pharmaceutical company executives know Michael Balls, a British zoologist and biology professor, as an outspoken opponent of animal laboratory testing.

7. Between the late 1970's and 1980's, Jamaican reggae musician Lone Ranger, born Anthony Alphonso Waldron, recorded nine albums.

8. In 2000, performance artist Jody Sperling founded Time Lapse Dance, a New York-based dance company whose mission is to provide modern reinterpretations of classic works.

9. People throughout the Middle East, Singapore, and Indonesia frequently eat Murtabak, a dish composed of mutton, garlic, egg, onion, and curry sauce.

10. Over the last thirty years, researchers have examined many forms of meditation and deemed a number of them ineffective.

Dangling Modifiers (p. 118), Suggested Answers

1. Characterized by scenes that are shot quickly and in real time, **guerilla filmmaking** is typically characterized by low budgets and simple props.

2. Located in the southern Andes and covered by glaciers, **Tronador** is an extinct volcano whose last eruption occurred many centuries ago.

3. Born in St. Lucia in the West Indies, **author Derek Walcott** work includes a number of plays and poems, most notably *Omeros*.

4. One of hundreds of islands that form the Indonesian archipelago, **Bali** is less than 100 miles wide, yet it holds within its borders a rich and dramatic history.

5. Historically based on the carving of walrus ivory, which was once found in abundance, **Inuit art** has, since the mid-twentieth century, also included prints and figures made from soft stone.

6. One of the greatest musicians of her time, **Clara Wieck** began piano studies when she was five years old; by the age of twelve she was renowned as both a performer and a composer.

7. Raised in Hong Kong and Shanghai before he moved to the United States, **I.M. Pei** has designed buildings that are immediately recognizable because of their characteristic glass exteriors and use of geometrical forms.

8. Correct

9. Though educated and well mannered, **Jane Eyre** remains of low status throughout the majority of the novel that bears her name.

10. Born at Dromoland Castle in County Clare, Ireland in 1821, **artist and engineer George O'Brien** had an aristocratic background that seemed to be at odds with his life in the Australian outback.

11. Correct

12. Despite winning several architectural awards, **the university's new dormitory** has been criticized by students for its impractical layout.

13. One of the earliest authorities to take a stand against pollution, **King Edward I** proclaimed in 1306 that sea coal could not be burned because the smoke it created was hazardous to people's health.

14. Predicting renewed interest in their country's natural resources, **political leaders** have established a plan to create mines in the most underdeveloped regions.

15. Having remained under Moorish rule until the twelfth century, **many Spaniards** still spoke Arabic when their cities first came under the control of European monarchs.

Misplaced Modifiers (p. 120)

1. The Spanish city of Valencia is the birthplace of horchata, a drink made from the juice of tiger nuts and said to date from the eighth century.

2. One of the most important poets of the Harlem Renaissance, Claude McKay moved to New York after studying agronomy in Kansas.

3. Founded by Leland Stanford, the California Street Cable Railroad is an established public transit company in San Francisco.

4. Correct

5. Praised by consumer magazines for being both versatile and affordable, the food processor performs a wide range of functions, including chopping, dicing, and pureeing, when a switch is flipped.

6. Fortresses protected many ancient cities from bands of invaders roaming in search of settlements to plunder.

7. Some of the world's fastest trains, which can reach speeds of up to 200 miles per hour, run between the cities of Tokyo and Kyoto.

8. Originally constructed during the Roman Republic, the House of Livia contains brightly colored frescoes that depict bucolic landscapes and mythological scenes and that date back to the first decades B.C.

9. The Georgian port of Batumi, which once housed some of the world's first oil pipelines, fell into decline in the mid-twentieth century.

10. The bass viol, which resembles the cello, has experienced a resurgence in popularity over the past several decades.

Parallel Structure II: Phrases (p. 123)

1. Correct

2. The figure skater was praised not only for her mastery of difficult technical skills **but also for the elegance and grace of her performance**.

3. While the novel has many detractors, it also has many admirers who argue that its popularity is based on its gripping storyline **and the believability of its characters' motives**.

4. Known for her musical compositions as well as for her poems and letters, Hildegard of Bingen was just as renowned in the twelfth century **as (she was) in** the twentieth.

5. The university is installing an electronic course-evaluation system so that students can decide whether they should register for certain classes **or avoid them altogether**.

6. For fans of the legendary food writer Charles H. Baker, the contents of a dish are **less compelling than the story behind it**.

7. During the sixteenth century, an outbreak of fighting in Europe led to the invention of new weapons **and to the growth and evolutions of old ones**.
8. Correct

9. The development of identity was one of psychologist Erik Erikson's greatest concerns, both in his own life **and in his theory**.

10. The bass clarinet, although similar to the more common soprano clarinet, is distinguished both by the greater length of its body **and by the presence of several additional keys**.

11. At its peak, the Roman army was nearly unconquerable because of the discipline of its soldiers, the hard and effective training of its commanders, **and the exceptional organization of its troops**.

12. Correct (it is unnecessary to repeat the verb *became* after the word *audience* to make the sentence parallel – the verb "applies" to both adjectives)

The Subjunctive (p. 125)

1. Correct

2. Incorrect (work)

3. Correct

4. Correct

5. Correct

6. Correct

7. Incorrect (had succeeded)

8. Incorrect (had not cleared)

9. Correct

10. Correct

Fixing Sentences Test (p. 131)

1. C: Gerund Required

2. B: Improper Gerund Use

3. D: Tense Consistency

4. C: Fragment/Non-Essential Clause

5. D: Parallel Structure

6. A: No Error

7. B: Dangling Modifier

8. E: Semicolon; Pronoun-Antecedent

9. E: Pronoun-Antecedent; Would vs. Will

10. C: Parallel Structure

11. D: Dangling Modifier

12. B: Missing Antecedent/Participle Required

13. A: No Error

14. E: Parallel Structure

Acknowledgments

I would like to thank Jean Hart for her extraordinary eye for detail and invaluable advice on content and style; Brian O'Connor for the many, many hours he spent formatting; and Debbie Stier for her unwavering support and enthusiasm. Without them, I might still be trying to finish this book. In addition, thanks to the Vadapalas family for allowing me nearly unlimited use of their computer when mine refused to cooperate; to Gabriella Luna and Francesca DiGirolamo for their time and input; to Ricardo Pascual for his suggestion that I include an index of College Board questions, and for being my unofficial proofreader; and to all of my students who patiently served as guinea pigs as I tried out various drafts of exercises. May you never have to look at another SAT Writing section again!

ABOUT THE AUTHOR

A graduate of Wellesley College, Erica Meltzer is based in New York City. She has worked as a tutor, test-writer, and blogger since 2007, helping students raise their SAT Critical Reading and Writing scores by hundreds of points. *The Ultimate Guide to SAT Grammar*, her first book, is currently used by tutors and tutoring companies across the United States. She is also the author *The Critical Reader: The Complete Guide to SAT Critical Reading* (2013), and you can visit her online at http://www.thecriticalreader.com.

Made in the USA
Middletown, DE
02 October 2014